DEDICATION

We would like to express our gratitude to our parents for their love, encouragement, and support. Also to our children, Ryan and Rania, for having to put up with us while this book was written.

TABLE OF CONTENTS

HOW TO TURN ANGER INTO LOVE
A Spiritual Guide

Reshmi M. Siddique, Ph.D.
Mahmood I. Siddique, D.O.

QualHealth Inc.
Lawrenceville, New Jersey

Important Note

The information presented in this book is of a general nature and meant to help the reader in their quest for spiritual healing. This book is sold with the understanding that the authors and publisher are not engaged in rendering medical or professional advice. The authors and publisher shall have no liability to any person or entity with respect to any loss or damage caused or alleged to be caused directly or indirectly by the information contained in this book. All names and identifying circumstances of case examples in this book have been changed beyond recognition to protect the privacy of the individuals. Any similarity of cases to reader experiences is purely coincidental.

How to Turn Anger into Love
by Reshmi M. Siddique, Ph.D.,
and Mahmood I. Siddique, D.O.
Copyright © 2004 by QualHealth Inc.

Published and distributed in the United States by:
QualHealth Inc.
P.O. Box 6539
Lawrenceville, NJ 08648

Publisher's Cataloging-in-Publication
Siddique, Reshmi M.
    How to turn anger into love : a spiritual guide /
Reshmi M. Siddique, Mahmood I. Siddique.
    p. cm.
    Includes bibliographical references and index.
    ISBN 1-932675-41-8
    LCCN 2003098217
    1. Anger.   2. Life skills.   3. Interpersonal
relations.   I. Siddique, Mahmood I.   II. Title.
BF575.A5S54 2004   152.4'7

INTRODUCTION

*A*nger is an unpleasant feeling. Many of us have been told in childhood that it is a "bad" emotion. Therefore, we keep this emotion inside of us without expressing it. Many of us, on the other hand, express it in harmful ways that destroy our relationships. The bottom line is that too often we don't know how to manage this feeling.

Anger, however, is more than simply a feeling. It can have a deadly physical impact on your health. You may not be aware of this, but if you don't learn to manage your anger and understand its significance, it can lead to a host of diseases. If you think that heart disease and cancer are mainly caused by food habits, genetics, or other lifestyle factors, think again. We will show that improperly managed anger is an independent risk factor for these two largest killer diseases.

You can diet or exercise as much as you want; however, if you can't manage your anger, whether it is impatience or outright rage, all your efforts can be useless. Plaque in your arteries will continue to build up, leading to a heart attack or stroke. Other serious ailments such as depression, asthma, and insomnia are also associated with anger. Part I of this book will review scientific information in the last 25 years on the link between anger and disease. It will help you understand why you need to take anger management very seriously. If you lose your health, you can lose everything in life. Health is the best wealth.

So, how do you turn anger into love? The answer to the question is a spiritual one. First you need to understand that you are part of an Infinite Intelligence that is composed of all love. Further, this love has many different elements, such as compassion, understanding, forgiveness, and creativity. Each of these love traits are like fragments of a broken pitcher that you need to pick up and glue back together to restore the pitcher.

Feelings of anger, if appropriately used, are like a magnet that can help you pick up these fragments. Your anger can then transform itself into love, which is the glue that seals all the fragments in place on the pitcher. Once your pitcher of life is restored and whole, it is able to hold the life-giving water of your divinity, which is love. The ultimate purpose of your life is that you should become a vessel of Love.

The word "heal" derives from the word "whole." You are healed when your pitcher of life is whole—spiritually, emotionally, and physically. In order to help you understand what it really means to be whole, Part I of this book will give you an idea of your purpose in life and your connection to Infinite Intelligence. The term "Infinite Intelligence" is the same as the Higher Power we often call God. We will also refer to it as the Universe, Spirit, and Love in this book.

Understanding anger is important for the journey of your spirit. The journey of your spirit is based on mystery. Solving the mystery means being keenly aware of and seeing the symbolic clues in the pattern of events that are woven in your daily life. Feelings of anger are clues to help you better understand yourself. They can inform you of who you are now and can help you transform yourself into who you want to be. Just like a caterpillar is transformed into a butterfly, your anger can transform itself into love. When you discover unconditional love, your soul will be able to fly in freedom to its destiny of divinity.

Transformation involves inner and outer change, usually beyond recognition. As your inner life changes beyond recognition, your outer life will do so accordingly. A key message of this book is that your outer life is always a reflection of your inner life. Your inner life, which is composed of thoughts and beliefs, is the creative vehicle of your experiences, which are aspects that you can always change.

Since you alone have the capacity to change your inner world, the importance of personal responsibility is a key take-away message of this book. If you want the world to change around you, you must change first. Your anger can be a pathway to this goal. It also can be the pathway to many other aspects of love. We will discuss this in Part II.

Transforming anger is not only about learning and reflecting the spiritual lessons of love. Transformation means taking practical steps to learn how to communicate compassionately when you are angry. It also means that you need to weave acts of kindness and meditation into your daily routine. Lastly, Mahmood, who is a sleep medicine physician, will inform you that your anger and irritability level have a lot to do with how well you sleep. Sleep health is one of the last pillars of medicine that is slowly beginning to shake off its slumber. Although you may not be aware of it, sleep health is just as vital to you as diet and exercise. Part III will highlight some of these practical steps in anger management.

This book was jointly created by Reshmi and Mahmood. Although Reshmi wrote the text, Mahmood contributed significantly to its development and content. The primary motivation for writing this book is that we wanted to share with you some of the principles we used to heal our own anger struggles. We have outlined these principles because they simply worked for *us* when we implemented them in our life.

A number of case examples are used in various parts of the book. To protect the privacy of all individuals, we changed all names and identifying details beyond recognition.

We sincerely hope you will find this book of value, not only to manage your own anger, but also to understand the importance of feelings in general. Too often we suppress our feelings and do not listen to them. Our feelings are the friends of our souls, always guiding and leading us to our true nature. We hope that through this book, we will be able to lead and guide you to your core of Love. If we do succeed, then we have practiced medicine in its highest form and fulfilled our earthly roles as healers.

If you wish to contact us, please do so at the address below. You can also check us out at our Web site, www.SleepHealthDoc.com.

With love,

Reshmi and Mahmood Siddique
P.O. Box 6539
Lawrenceville, NJ 08648

$\mathscr{P}$ART I

Understanding How Anger Can Either Heal or Hurt You

1

THE RIVER OF ANGRY FEELINGS

here are basically two types of human feelings: pleasant and unpleasant. The purpose of any feeling is to provide a barometer of where you are emotionally and spiritually and to guide your choices for a peaceful life. A choice is a thought. Any choice that you make will have a feeling attached to it. If that choice feels good, then it is the right choice for you and for all who are affected by it. If it does not feel good, then it is not the right choice. A feeling is an emotion, which is energy in motion.

Anger is an emotion that does not feel pleasant. We can think of it as a river. Sometimes it rages past us in a sweeping current. At other times, it spurts out on the banks of our minds in annoyance and impatience. Too often, we get drowned in its whirlpools, or we dam the flow. Over time, damming it only leads to a burst in the floodgates of our rage, so that we get carried away and swallowed up in its torrents. Whichever way this feeling expresses itself within us, it usually is a signal that something is not right in our lives.

A river always flows to the ocean. The destination of our river of anger is the Ocean of Love. Another name for the Ocean of Love is Infinite Intelligence or Spirit. This book will teach you how to peacefully sail on your river of anger, so that you can safely reach this Ocean. It will make you aware of how you can navigate through the perilous and torrid currents of your anger without getting drowned. This book will give you the compass of spiritual understanding, as well as the oars of practicality, to steer the boat of your soul calmly in the disturbed waters of anger.

We often think our anger is "bad" only because we get drowned in it and do not know how to navigate through it. We can think differently, however, and not allow our anger to drown us. A river is water that flows. Water can be life-giving or life-threatening. It is our *choice* regarding how we want to experience it. This book will help you make these life-giving choices, so that you may view your anger as a passageway to peace and love.

All of us want peace in our lives. A balance in the spiritual, mental, and physical areas of our lives characterizes this state of peace. Feelings of anger play an important role in helping us to see where we are not in balance in our lives, or what areas we need to work on. The important point is not to deny these feelings. We need to acknowledge these feelings and to express them in ways that meet our own needs without harming or hurting others.

Often anger is associated with some sort of underlying pain or suffering such as hurt, jealousy, stress, or being offended. Whatever specific form the suffering takes, the root cause of all human suffering is that most of us think we are separate from each other, and that we are not divine beings.

Our egos like to convince us that we are separate and different from each other. In other words: "I" am different and better than "you"; therefore, "I" need to have "my" way or prove that "I" am right and "you" are wrong. Our ego is the same thing as our self-image, which believes in separation. Its function is to create an illusion that we are not connected to each other.

Further, the ego believes that it is not connected to Infinite Intelligence, the Higher Power, which is the source of all creative energy. You can see this illustrated in Figure 1. It is from this illusion of separation that fear and doubt come into our hearts, which leads to unloving thoughts and actions against others. These unloving thoughts and actions form the basis of anger.

Ego Idea of Infinite Intelligence

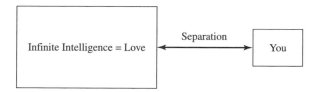

Fig. 1. *Ego's idea is that you and other human beings are separate from each other and from Infinite Intelligence, which is all love. Your anger can bridge this gap of separation by bringing you closer and closer to Infinite Intelligence, until you believe that you are a part of Infinite Intelligence.*

If your feelings are truly a barometer to help you assess the state of your emotional and spiritual well-being, then feelings of anger can tell you what is wrong with your life and where you need to heal. As we mentioned earlier in the introduction of this book, the word "heal" derives from the word "whole." Your anger can help you integrate or make "whole" your spirit, mind, and body. From the perspective of Figure 1, you are healed when you are inside the box of Infinite Intelligence rather than outside the box. We will show you later how your anger can help you bridge this gap.

From our river analogy, we heal ourselves when we change our perception of anger from an emotion of disturbance to an emotion of peace. Healing occurs when we use our river of anger to cleanse and purify ourselves. Our anger becomes transformed when our soul journey changes from a tumultuous one to a calm one. We reach peace and tranquility when our individual soul comes in union with Infinite Intelligence. This is the true meaning of transformation.

Transformation, however, may not happen overnight. It is a process that could take a lifetime. This process is also known as spiritual growth. Whenever we are stirred up in anger or irritability, it is a sign from the Universe that our soul is ready for more growth toward divinity. It is a wake up call that we need to do more work on ourselves. The purpose of traveling on a different river of anger is to learn some new aspect of Love that we were not aware of. It could be compassion, forgiveness, patience, or another virtue. This book will lead you in this journey.

Angry feelings can guide us to see where we need to heal.

2

DROWNING IN THE
ANGER OF DISEASE:

How Anger Can Lead to Illness

*W*hen we habitually deny our anger, or are not willing to confront the underlying issues beneath it, it is like getting drowned in the river of this emotion. When we are not willing to use anger as an opportunity for spiritual growth, it may express itself physically in the form of disease. A disease is the body telling you that it is not at ease.

A disease also indicates that you need to pay attention to the unresolved emotional and spiritual issues that are underlying that pain and discomfort. In the following sections, we will discuss some thought-provoking, patient-specific examples to show you the link between anger and disease. All identifying details have been changed to protect the privacy of these individuals. We will then discuss the medical and public health research on this link.

THE CASE OF CANCEROUS CAMELIA

Camelia, a 70-year-old patient of Mahmood, was diagnosed with cancer. She never smoked, was physically active, and had an excellent healthy diet throughout her life. Further, she did not have any family history of cancer. How then, did she get cancer? It is not certain. We do know, however, that over the course of 50 years of marriage, she hardly expressed her feelings during an argument or "fight." She had been taught by her parents that speaking up against a husband was not the "proper" and "ladylike" thing to do. Often, any angry expression from her husband was met with silence on her side, even if her husband was wrong. For all practical purposes, these were one-sided fights.

In addition to not expressing her true feelings to her husband, she spent all her life taking care of others at the expense of herself. It would be hard to believe that she did not have any resentment towards her spouse and her self-negating lifestyle. It is more than likely that her deep-seated resentment played a role in her illness. Although this patient was able to have a successful mastectomy (surgical removal of breasts), whether or not the cancer recurs remains to be seen.

Modern medical science has focused on the physical causes of cancer such as carcinogens and other "risk factors" such as smoking, starchy diets, genetic history, and other environmental hazards. While some of these factors certainly may play a role in causing cancer, let us not forget the role of our emotions and the effect they have on our bodies. If it is true that human beings are literally bundles of energy, whereby every thought and emotion has a physical impact, then the energy of resentment can easily take bodily expression in the form of cancer or other disease.

THE CASE OF INFLAMMATORY IAN

Another patient, Ian, had a condition known as psoriasis, which is an inflammatory skin disorder that is characterized by red, patchy, swollen "bumps" on the skin. This patient was able to see a direct link between unexpressed angry feelings and worsening conditions in his psoriasis. These unexpressed feelings would usually occur when he had disagreements with his boss. Because he did not have the courage to express his angry feelings directly to his boss, the patches of redness and thickness would literally become bumpy and swollen. Angry feelings caused the inflammation. The swollen bumps stored the angry feelings in these areas of his skin.

FEVER IN THE FAMILY

On a personal note, we know that our own anger as parents can end up as physical disease in our children. We have seen this happen when we tried to deny the underlying issues which anger was trying to teach us.

Often when we had an angry exchange between ourselves, either our son or our daughter ended up getting a fever on that particular day, or shortly following that. In fact, the pattern was **consistent.** The second thing we realized about this pattern was that the **intensity** and **length** of the children's fever varied, depending on how quickly we, the parents, were able to take responsibility for our anger and learn the associated spiritual lesson. The more quickly we were able to take responsibility, the milder and shorter the fever.

Fever and high temperature are symbolic of anger. Germs such as viruses and bacteria actually don't "cause" disease. The body also has to allow the germ to enter and multiply to lead to a full-blown disease. It appears in our case, the anger response created energy "leaks" in our children's bodies, which allowed the germs to enter and manifest as disease.

Scientific Studies on How Anger Is Related to Disease

The purpose of this section is to give you a view of the clinical and public health[1] studies on how anger is related to physical disease. **It is important for you to be aware of how anger can literally *kill* and lead to serious illness if you do not know how to harness and use its energy.** This is the key take-away message for this section. We will focus on cardiovascular disease, depression, cancer, asthma, and insomnia. **Some of these diseases are leading**

---

[1]Public health research refers to the study of diseases in large sections of the population. A focus of public health research is to determine how many people have a certain disease at a point in time (prevalence) and how many new cases of that disease occur (incidence).

killers and may have *nothing to do with diet and exercise.* **Treatment and prevention of these diseases, therefore, need to consider** *spiritual and emotional healing as part of a comprehensive
medical program.* We chose these diseases for discussion because
we have a professional interest in them.

Anger may certainly be related to a host of other diseases, but
it is not possible to discuss every type of disease in this book. As
each disease section is self-contained, you may pick and choose
sections you are interested in, and go on to the next chapter, which
discusses anger in the context of the purpose of your life.

Cardiovascular Disease and Anger
Cardiovascular diseases (CVDs) refer to diseases involving the
flow and circulation of our blood system, such as coronary heart
disease and stroke. According to the American Heart Association,
more than 61 million Americans have one or more types of cardiovascular disease. Of these types, coronary heart disease is the
single largest killer of both men and women.

Far from being a "man's disease," almost 236,000 U.S.
women die each year due to heart disease, which is more than all
types of cancer combined; indeed, a **woman is twice as likely to
die from heart disease than all cancers combined, and 10 times
more likely to die from heart disease than breast cancer.** The
sad truth is that a recent Gallup poll found that 4 out of 5 women
are not even aware that heart disease is the leading cause of death.
Since 1984, heart attacks and other CVDs have killed more women
than men, and the gap is widening each year.

Coronary heart disease (CHD) mainly includes heart attack
and chest pain. The function of our heart is to pump blood through
our body. Our arteries are "pipes" which carry our blood to the
heart. We have heart disease when our heart pump does not work
very well, or when the lining of our arteries becomes clogged with
excessive material such as cholesterol. Cholesterol is a waxy substance in the bloodstream that cannot be dissolved. If too much of

it circulates in the bloodstream, it can form plaque or hard deposits on the arteries, which can clog them.

A myocardial infarction (MI) is a heart attack. It happens when the blood supply to part of the heart muscle (myocardium) is severely reduced or stopped. This may happen because one or more of the arteries supplying blood to the heart may be blocked. The heart muscles become damaged and, therefore, cannot pump blood. Heart disease is also characterized by angina, which is chest pain or discomfort due to insufficient blood flow to the heart muscle.

A recent study which reviewed almost 45 studies on the link between anger, hostility, and CHD came to the conclusion that **angry and hostile people, in general, are more prone to heart disease than those who are not habitually angry.** Although the exact biological mechanism by which anger influences heart disease is not known, there are some plausible hypotheses.

One hypothesis is that **anger releases chemicals known as catecholamines.** Research has demonstrated that too much of these chemicals circulating in our bodies can directly damage the heart muscle, as well as play a role in the development of atherosclerotic lesions (patches of fatty and other "undesirable" matter that build up in the muscular linings of the arteries). These lesions, in turn, play a role in causing a heart attack.

In many of the existing studies, anger has been measured by the way it is expressed. "Anger out" refers to the tendency to respond with verbal and physical aggression. **The vocal expression of anger refers to anger taking the form of loud, rapid, and interruptive speech. Research has shown that this kind of expression by itself is responsible for causing a negative reaction on the cardiovascular system, which plays a role in heart disease.**

As we will discuss in Part III, one part of anger management is to learn how to speak in an even-toned voice. If we can learn how to express our angry feelings without aggression, and with a normal voice, this by itself will not produce negative changes in our body chemicals which lead to heart disease.

"Anger-in" refers to actively withholding or inhibiting anger, and has been shown to increase the risk of heart disease. This was found in the well-known Framingham Heart Study, which followed 1,674 individuals over an eight-year period. This study found that **both men and women who** *suppressed* **their anger were at increased risk of developing heart disease compared to those who did not suppress their anger.** This study was also the first study to look at Type A behavior in women. Type A behavior is characterized by impatience, a chronic sense of hurry, hostility, and competitiveness.

The Framingham Study found that women who had Type A behavior were twice as likely to develop heart disease compared to women who did not have Type A behavior (i.e., Type B women). Further, whether they were working women or housewives, they had a similar chance of developing heart disease. **Research since the Framingham Study has provided evidence that the** *component of anger and hostility* **within Type A behavior may be responsible for the increased risk of heart disease.**

If you are frequently angry, what is the chance that you will develop CHD? Many studies have looked at this, but we will discuss a fairly recent one conducted by Dr. Janice Williams and her colleagues published in the medical journal *Circulation*. **This study found that people who had normal blood pressure, but with high anger, were twice as likely to develop overall heart disease than those who had low anger. Further, the chance of getting a heart attack was almost three times greater for those with high anger compared to those who had low anger.**

Like many other previous studies, anger was measured in the Williams study by a questionnaire known as the Spielberger Trait Anger Scale, developed by researchers from the University of South Florida. This questionnaire assesses anger on a four-point scale: almost never = 1; sometimes = 2; often = 3; and almost always = 4. The higher the score, the angrier the person is. The anger score (ranging from 10 to 40) is obtained by summing each of the individual items. In the study by Dr. Williams, scores of

- 22 to 40 define high anger;
- 15 to 21 define moderate anger; and
- 10 to 14 define low anger.

The following are the 10 questions in this anger scale:

1. I am quick tempered.
2. I have a fiery temper.
3. I am a hotheaded person.
4. I get angry when I am slowed down by others' mistakes.
5. I feel annoyed when I am not given recognition for doing good work.
6. I "fly off the handle."
7. When I get angry, I say nasty things.
8. It makes me furious when I am criticized in front of others.
9. When I get frustrated, I feel like hitting someone.
10. I feel infuriated when I do a good job and get a poor evaluation.

The current research, therefore, indicates that there is nothing wrong with angry feelings per se; *how* we express them and *whether* we express them are the key factors determining our chances of developing heart disease. It is not surprising that anger is related to heart disease. Our heart is a symbol of love. Habitual anger that is not used for spiritual healing and transformation symbolizes the lack of love for others and ourselves. A heart attack symbolically means that love has been wounded or "attacked."

Research has also demonstrated that anger is related to stroke. A stroke occurs when a blood vessel that brings oxygen to the brain is clogged or bursts. Without oxygen, nerve cells in the brain cannot work and die within minutes. When these nerve cells do not work, the part of the body they control cannot work either, which often leads to paralysis. Stroke is the third largest cause of death in the United States. Although more men have strokes than women, women account for about 60 percent of all stroke deaths.

A 1999 study published in the medical journal *Stroke* found that men who expressed their anger outwardly when provoked were twice as likely to experience a stroke over an 8-year period compared to men who were more even-tempered. These results held true even after taking into account known risk factors such as smoking, blood pressure, and alcohol consumption. Although this was the first public health study to examine the relationship between stroke and anger, it was limited to only men. Further research needs to be undertaken to determine the relationship of anger and stroke in women.

Depression and Anger

Depression is a chronic disorder with symptoms ranging from low moods and irritability to thoughts of suicide. It can have a devastating effect not only on the lives of the sufferers, but also on their families and friends. Nearly 19 million people suffer from serious mood disorders each year in America. Of this number, almost 18 million people experience an episode of depression.

Women experience depression at roughly twice the rate of men. One-third of the population will have at least a mild episode of depression during their lifetimes, and about 15 percent of the general public will suffer from a major depressive disorder sometime in their lives. Less than half of all depressed persons are diagnosed each year. Only about one in 10 people suffering from depression receive adequate treatment. The worst consequence of untreated major depressive disorder is suicide.

Sigmund Freud, the popular psychiatrist, suggested that depression is anger turned inwards. A number of studies in the last 30 years have supported this hypothesis. These studies have shown that although depressed and nondepressed people report roughly equivalent levels of anger expression, **depressed people felt angrier and suppressed their anger more.**

One hypothesis for anger suppression in depressed people is that they are fearful of the consequences of anger expression, especially if they have expressed their anger in destructive ways in the past. These destructive anger expressions are known as "anger attacks," which are intense rage reactions that are associated with feelings of loss of control. Additionally, many depressed people deliberately suppress their feelings in an effort to maintain intimate relationships.

Although many of the existing studies have shown an association between anger and depression, these studies have not shown that anger actually *causes* depression. It is very possible that depression itself could cause the anger. A study in the *Journal of Nervous and Mental Diseases,* published in 1999, demonstrated that a group of recovered, depressed people reported more anger suppression and more fear of anger expression than did a similar group of never-depressed patients. The implication of this study was that anger was a likely cause of their depression.

The study just mentioned used a questionnaire known as "Silencing the Self Scale," which measures how feelings, including angry ones, are suppressed in order to maintain intimacy. Researchers from Harvard Medical School and Western Washington University developed this questionnaire. Sample questions are:

1. I tend to judge myself by how I think other people see me.
2. Considering my needs to be as important as those of the people I love is selfish.
3. I don't speak my feelings in an intimate relationship when I know they will cause disagreement.
4. I feel that my partner does not know my real self.
5. Often I look happy enough on the outside, but inwardly I am angry and rebellious.

This questionnaire is based on a 5-point scale, ranging from 1, which indicates strong disagreement, to 5, which represents strong agreement. The higher the score, the less often a person is willing to talk about their feelings. This study demonstrated that the group who had recovered from depression endorsed more of these attitudes than those who were never depressed.

While some studies have shown a relationship between inward-directed hostility and depression, other studies have shown depression to be linked with *overt* expression of anger. The level of anger experience can partly explain the fact that some depressed patients are overtly hostile, while others suppress their anger; for example, moderate anger may tend to be suppressed, whereas severe anger may tend to result in overt expression.

It should be mentioned that anger-associated depression is linked with hardening of the arteries in women. A recent study in *Psychosomatic Medicine* demonstrated that women with anger-associated depression were two-and-a-half times more likely to smoke than women with the least depression symptoms. Depressed women were also less likely to exercise or be physically fit than nondepressed women.

In this study, clinical hostility was associated with smoking and lower high-density lipoproteins (the good kind of cholesterol), both of which can lead to heart disease. In fact, hostility and anger go hand in hand. From a practical standpoint it is difficult to measure the two concepts separately. Hostility consists of negative beliefs about others, including cynicism and mistrust.

Cynicism refers to the belief that others are motivated by selfish concerns, and mistrust is the belief that others are likely to be hurtful. As we will show you in the next chapter, hostility and anger stem from a sense of fear that we are all separate. We will argue that in reality this is not true, as we are in fact part of an intelligent, universal energy.

Cancer and Anger

Cancer is the second leading cause of death in the United States, exceeded only by heart disease. One out of every four deaths is from cancer, with more than 1,500 people dying each day from the disease. According to the American Cancer Society, in the year 2002, almost 1,284,900 new cases of cancer will be diagnosed, with females accounting for half of these cases.

Almost one third of all female cases are from breast cancer, followed by cancers of the digestive system (e.g., stomach and colon) and lungs. Prostrate cancer represents the single largest category for men, followed by cancers of the digestive system and lungs.

Cancer is characterized by the spread and uncontrolled growth of abnormal cells. If the spread of these cells is not controlled, they can lead to death. External factors such as the use of tobacco, exposure to chemicals, radiation, obesity, and physical inactivity may cause cancer; internal factors, however, such as inherited mutations or suppressed immune conditions may also lead to the disease.

A number of studies to date have suggested that certain personality characteristics may be associated with suppressing the immune system, which may lead to the growth of cancer cells. This type of personality is known as "Type C." **The Type C individual is characterized as being unassertive, someone who tries to please others, is unexpressive of negative emotions, and is compliant with external authorities.**

In the late 1980s, Lydia Temoshok of the University of California School of Medicine did a review of studies exploring the relationship between personality, emotion, and cancer. In her review she found that **within the Type C personality, it was the emotion of anger that played a lead role in the cancer process.**

In particular, it was the inability of Type C individuals to express their anger that played a role in cancer initiation and progression. In her review, for example, she found that breast cancer patients were less able to express their anger than healthy women, or even women with fibrocystic (fiber-like, abnormal growth) disease. Further, they had a difficult time demonstrating their feelings and were not assertive.

A 1981 study by researchers Morris and Greer **found, on the other hand, that expressing anger through "anger attacks" was more common in breast cancer patients than in women with benign breast disease.** In this study, "extreme expressers" were individuals who had frequent temper outbursts and rarely concealed their feelings.

Although many of the existing studies show that anger is linked to cancer, they do not necessarily prove that anger actually caused the cancer. A few studies though, in the last two decades, have sought to show that anger maybe causally related to cancer. Research has shown that anger suppression may lead to a suppression of the immune system. When that happens, white blood cells (our fighter and protector cells) are not strong enough to fight cancer cells, which may in turn lead to a full-blown disease.

Cancer cells are in our bodies all the time; however, white blood cells in a healthy immune system normally destroy them before they have a chance to develop into deadly tumors. When the immune system is weakened, this cannot happen. Other studies have suggested that anger suppression may lead to increased levels of corticosteroids, which have shown to lead to a growth of cancerous cells.

Asthma and Anger
Asthma is a condition that affects the lungs. The most common feature of the disease is that the linings of the airways in the lungs become inflamed. In other words, the airway lining swells and becomes narrow. When this happens, it becomes very difficult for a person to breathe. When the airways of the lungs become inflamed, they also become highly sensitive to normally harmless substances. These are known as triggers.

In addition to the inflammation, the airways also become obstructed or partly blocked because of a tightness of the muscle linings. Almost 15 million individuals are affected by asthma in the United States, of which 10 million are adults. More than 500,000 hospitalizations and 5,000 deaths occur each year due to this condition.

In addition to environmental and physical triggers, such as allergens, air pollution, and cigarette smoke, emotional triggers such as anger can have a serious impact on causing an asthma attack, or making one worse. A study in 1987 by Howard Friedman of the University of California found that **the angrier and more hostile the person was, the worse his or her asthmatic response was.** What is interesting is that this study showed that the association of anger and asthma was even stronger than the association of anger and heart disease.

A more recent review of the literature in 1998 by Dr. Paul Lehrer of Robert Wood Johnson Medical School in New Jersey found that anger was associated with worsening asthma among individuals who were vulnerable. This review showed that **anger had even a greater impact on asthma than fear.** One way which anger may trigger asthma is through the nervous system. Since nerves are linked to the lungs, any emotional trigger such as anger could have an impact on agitating nerves in the airway linings, which in turn cause the airways to become tight (bronchoconstriction).

It is also important to note that the *memory* of anger can have an effect on asthma. A study by Ada Tal and Donald Miklich, published in *Psychosomatic Medicine* in 1976, found that among 10- to 15-year-old asthmatic children, a recollection of angry incidents had an impact on triggering asthma.

In particular, this study found that forced expiratory volume (FEV_1) actually decreased during recollection of anger incidents. FEV_1 is the amount of air one can forcefully exhale in 1 second after breathing in fully. Asthmatics generally have lower FEV_1

than persons without asthma because the amount of air they can exhale is less. Similar to other studies, this study also showed anger had a greater impact on asthma than fear.

If we look at asthma from a spiritual standpoint, the inflammation of the airways is symbolic of anger being stored, pent-up, or expressed in inappropriate ways. Suppressing our anger or expressing it in hurtful ways inhibits our ability to breathe the full potentiality of life.

Insomnia and Anger

Another symptom of anger is the condition of sleeplessness or insomnia. Difficulty falling asleep, staying asleep, or getting up too early are some of the key features of insomnia. A recent study found that the average American gets only 5½ hours of sleep a night, whereas the National Sleep Foundation recommends that humans need at least 8 hours of sleep for healthy functioning. Further, this survey found that only one out of four Americans rated their sleep quality as excellent or very good.[2]

While lack of sleep can impair short-term memory, alertness, and concentration, it can also slow the body's ability to fight disease and repair tissue, as well as increase the chances of being in an accident. In extreme cases, lack of sleep can cause premature death. Although many of us think that our sleep is expendable and we can "tough it out," lack of sleep can have serious long-term consequences for our physical health.

While insomnia may be caused by physical factors such as excess caffeine, alcohol consumption, or cigarette smoking, emotional factors may also play a role. A study by Anthony Kales and his colleagues, published in the *Archives of General Psychiatry* in 1976, found that insomniacs had a tendency to not express their

---

[2]Please visit our Web site, www.SleepHealthDoc.com to get your free special report on how to get quality sleep for good health.

feelings, such as anger. **This study found that among the many emotional factors that were measured in this study, depression and inhibited anger scored the highest.** As we said before, depression is anger turned inward. Apprehensive worrying is also another important emotional factor in insomniacs. More recent studies have supported these findings.

A study by Bonnet and Arand, published in 1997 in *Psychosomatic Medicine,* compared the emotional qualities of insomniacs with normal sleepers. **This study found that insomniacs were more depressed, angry, and confused than normal sleepers.** In fact, insomniac patients were three times more depressed and two times angrier than normal sleepers.

The purpose of this chapter on the link between anger and disease is to show you that if feelings of anger are either suppressed or expressed in harmful ways, they can easily lead to life-threatening diseases. The big question is: How do we use this powerful feeling for our spiritual growth (and hence for our true fulfillment and happiness), rather than allowing it to cause physical ailments, and even death?

We will show in the next few chapters how our feelings of anger can serve an important purpose by leading us towards our divinity; how we can become *aware* of these feelings and *know* how to apply them to spiritual development. The purpose of this book is to give you the awareness of choice as well as the knowledge of how to do this. An important part of this understanding is the knowledge that we are a part of a universal flow of life.

Anger that is suppressed or expressed in harmful ways may lead to physical disease.

3

MERGING WITH THE OCEAN OF LOVE:

The Purpose of Your Life

*D*o you know your purpose in life? Why are you here on this planet Earth? The answers to these questions are spiritual in nature. You will not be able to use your anger to help you heal unless you really know and understand the answers to these important questions. Our task is to help you understand what your purpose in life is, so that you will be able to effectively manage your anger and use it for your growth.

In simple terms, the purpose of your life is to realize that you are a divine being who is literally a part of all humanity. From an energy, quantum physics standpoint, there is no difference between you and the rest of humanity. The purpose of life, then, is to break down the mask of illusion that you are separate from other human beings and Infinite Intelligence itself. Your emotions, including your anger, are vehicles that can help you towards this realization.

We noted in Chapter 1 that our anger was like a river. The natural course of a river is to flow towards the ocean. Similarly, our river of anger will gravitationally flow to the Ocean of Love. Another term for this Ocean of Love is Infinite Intelligence. Our river will carry us down to the Ocean, so that we will eventually merge with it.

When we merge with the Ocean, we realize that every drop of water in the Ocean is exactly the same as another drop. Each drop is like an individual soul. The Ocean is all souls joined together. This is the nature of Infinite Intelligence. When you have merged with the Ocean of Love, you will have realized what your purpose in life is. In other words, you will have achieved union or yoga in the broadest sense of the term.

Looking at it from another way, your job is to convince your ego to get inside the box of Infinite Intelligence as in Figure 1 in Chapter 1. **In reality you are already a part of this Intelligence,** *but you may not be aware of it.* **The purpose of your life is to close the gap of separation between your false illusion of your self-image and your true nature as a divine being. You have to learn to be aware (and really believe) that you are a divine being.**

From a practical standpoint you can use your anger to bring you closer to your source of Infinite Intelligence by allowing yourself to learn the different lessons of love. Note that Infinite Intelligence is nothing other than love. Therefore, in order to realize your divinity, you will need to learn all the elements of love, so that you become whole and realize your infinite potential. We will show you in Part II that your anger will be able to teach you some of the following important lessons of love:

- Personal responsibility and **your role as cocreator** of all your life experiences
- Knowing how to **love yourself**
- **Freedom from false beliefs** which are inner addictions
- **Prosperity consciousness,** in terms of comfort, loving relationships, financial wealth, and peace of mind
- A healthy **balanced lifestyle** where you have your priorities in life right
- **Creative growth** to enable you to be better than you used to be
- **Compassion and understanding**

- **Present moment awareness**
- **Unconditional love**

If you truly listen to your feelings of anger and take appropriate actions, it will lead to compassionate choice and true fulfillment. If, on the other hand, you do not listen to the messages of your anger, it will only lead to more anger and pain.

The purpose of life is to recognize that we are part of the Divine and that we are not separate from any other human being. Our anger can help us achieve this understanding if we choose to.

4

UNDERSTANDING YOUR CONNECTION TO INFINITE INTELLIGENCE

*I*n the previous chapters, we mentioned the fact that all of us are part of Infinite Intelligence. As you read those sections you (your mind and ego) might have wondered, "This does not make logical sense. I don't see how I am another person when my body is clearly separate and fixed in time and space. It also does not make sense that I am a part of Infinite Intelligence. I always thought that this Higher Power was outside of me."

In this chapter we are going to convince your mind with scientific arguments that you are indeed a part of a oneness. Your eyes might see things as solid and separate, but the true nature of your reality is invisible energy. Most of your anger is based on a perception of someone hurting you in some way. This stems from a belief that you are separate from that person. We will show you through scientific logic that you are not separate from Infinite Intelligence, or any other human being. Understanding the logic behind this will help you in a number of ways:

- You will get a better understanding of the universal **law of cause and effect,** which states that what you get in life (effect) is due to what you put in (cause). Another term for this is, "you reap what you sow." You will, therefore, see how you can literally "attract" angry situations into your life by your thoughts and words if you are not careful.

Conversely, you will be able to see how to use your anger for your growth.

- You will realize that you are a **cocreator of your life's experiences,** both good and bad. It will make you more conscious of the need for personal responsibility in your life's affairs.
- You will be able to see **everyone, including those who anger you, as Spirit in material disguise.** You will, therefore, learn to be careful to not shoot the Spiritual messenger.

One of the most eloquent spokespersons in the last decade who has been able to provide scientific logic to the notion that we are one is best-selling author and physician, Dr. Deepak Chopra. Dr. Chopra's insights are based on a combination of quantum physics and Ayurvedic medicine. In the next few paragraphs we will summarize some of the key ideas that he has written about.

Ayurveda (meaning literally, "science of life") is essentially **mind/body medicine,** which is a part of alternative medicine. As a side note, it is interesting to note that 80 percent of the world's population uses complementary and alternative medicine therapies. In the United States, it is estimated that 42 percent of the public use alternative medicine approaches for their personal healthcare needs.

Given the growing importance alternative medicine, the U.S. government set up the National Center for Complementary and Alternative Medicine, whose purpose is to support scientific research in alternative medicine therapies including Ayurveda. The basic idea of Ayurveda is two-fold:

1. **The Universe and its inherent creative intelligence is an** *extension of you.*
2. **Your mind, which produces thoughts, is the creative vehicle that has an impact on your body; i.e., what you think about has an effect on your body.**

Quantum physics relies on the idea that the basic unit of all things material is the quanta, which is invisible energy. In fact our bodies, which seem so solid, are really intelligent energy. The same thing is true for all the stars, planets, and galaxies. In fact, all of material nature, including humankind, is condensed energy. Further, we share the same one energy, known in modern science as the unified field.

As you can see from the descriptions of Ayurveda and quantum physics, they are saying the same thing: **Infinite Intelligence is one unified field of creative and universal intelligence, and we as humans are a part of this divinity.** In other words, we are not separate from each other, as our ego would like to think. According to Dr. Chopra, you are a "quantum mechanical body." The implication of this is:

- **Your body is *not* fixed in time and space,** as conventional medicine would like you to believe; rather, it is a flowing intelligence of energy that does not have any fixed boundaries. It is a scientific fact that 99.9 percent of the atoms of your "solid" body are recycled within a year. You might look the same, but in reality from an energy standpoint you are a different person.
- **Your thoughts are vibrations of energy in the quantum field,** which can create a physical impact on your body and have an effect on your immediate environment. It is a scientific fact, for example, that if you have a loving thought, your body will produce healing chemicals known as endorphins. In Chapter 2, we showed that if you have angry thoughts, your body could produce damaging chemicals known as catecholamines.
- There is a part of you that controls your mind and is the source of all life; popularly this is known as the **soul** or **spirit.**

This description of the quantum mechanical body implies that your body, mind, and soul are one unit. In order to help you understand how you are connected to Infinite Intelligence, consider Figure 2. It

Infinite Intelligence and How You Are Connected to It

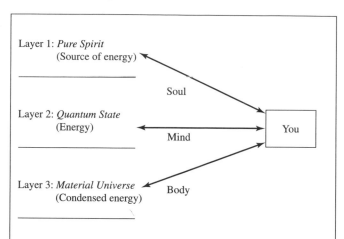

*Fig. 2.   You are contained in the big outer box representing Infinite Intelligence, which is composed of three different layers. You are, therefore, a **part** of Infinite Intelligence. You are linked by your soul to Pure Spirit, which is the source of all energy. Your mind is linked to the quantum energy field through thoughts. Finally, your body is part of the material universe.*

shows that you are a unit (shown here as the smaller box) that is contained in the larger box of Infinite Intelligence. **Note that the small box and large box comprise *one single unit.***

Layer 1 of the Infinite Intelligence box in Figure 2 is comprised of Pure Spirit, which you can think of as the infinite source of all creative energy. In this state there is no energy, but a silent, timeless Being who is fully conscious and wants to express itself. You can think of Pure Spirit as a choreographer of a dance who has an image of how he wants the dance to materialize. You are linked to Pure Spirit by your soul. You can also think of your soul as a silent observer.

Layer 2 is the quantum energy field. Dr. Chopra likes to call this the "transition zone." This state is dominated by waves and particles that come in and out of existence, depending on how much focus and attention Pure Spirit gives. It is in this state where Pure Spirit, like a choreographer, is thinking about how a dance should be orchestrated and gives directions to the dancers, who start practicing for the final performance.

You are linked to this state by all the thoughts that your mind generates. You cannot generate anything physical in the world unless you have a thought first. A thought is nothing other than quantum fluctuations of intelligent energy. In other words, **thoughts have the power to create your physical reality. The more you think of something, the more likely it will materialize in the physical world.**

Layer 3 is the material universe, which we perceive with our five senses. In this state, an idea or image that took shape in the state of Pure Spirit and the quantum energy field finally takes on a physical reality of its own. While things may appear to be solid and hard, including our bodies, they are in fact pure energy as we mentioned before. While our physical senses tell us we are separate, this is really an illusion, because in reality we are different forms of the same one universal energy. Taking the metaphor of the dance to completion, it is in the physical universe that the performance of the dance finally happens.

In summary, **Infinite Intelligence is composed of three parts that form one whole:** (1) the choreographer who does not do the dance (source of energy); (2) the process of orchestration (energy); and finally, (3) the dance performance itself (condensed energy). **Further, you are contained within this oneness of Infinite Intelligence.**

Another simple analogy, which summarizes the description of Infinite Intelligence, is a painting. Imagine that Infinite Intelligence *is* a landscape painting. A painting is composed of many different parts. You can think of the Pure Spirit part of Infinite Intelligence as a blank canvas with nothing on it. As Pure Spirit wants to express itself, it sends out vibrations and thoughts in the quantum field. You can think of this process as the individual brush strokes of paint on the canvas. Each thought you have is like an individual brush stroke.

As this energy becomes denser and turns into matter, you can draw the analogy that individual brush strokes form to create two-dimensional objects such as trees and animals in the landscape. In the end, you will have a fully completed painting.

The important point to realize is this: The blank canvas, the individual brush strokes, and the objects, which were created by the brush strokes, form to create a whole picture. Each element of the picture is necessary to create a vision of a landscape. Similarly, Infinite Intelligence is Pure Spirit, quantum energy, and the physical universe, **all in one.**

After reading this you might be saying to yourself that you were taught in your religious tradition of an Infinite Intelligence who is "out there," and separate from you. The deeper, however, you study the world's religions, especially the monotheistic ones, you will see that there is no conflict with what modern science has revealed. At one level or another, virtually all the major religions describe God as an infinite being who is also omnipresent.

Omnipresent means to be everywhere at the same time. It means universal. If Infinite Intelligence is everywhere, then it must be in all of us at the same time. There is not any place where it cannot be. Omnipresence also implies that God is indivisible (something you cannot divide into pieces). Omnipresence and oneness as described in traditional religions is the same thing as the unified field as described by modern science.

In summary, you are connected and a part of Infinite Intelligence. While you are physically here in the material universe, your mind is connected to the quantum energy field through your thoughts. Your soul is a part of Pure Spirit that is eternal and the unchanging source of all creative energy. **The most important point to note is that by being connected to the Infinite, you**

determine your own destiny. This naturally brings us to the next chapter, which shows you the power of your thoughts, and how you can use them as tools to create and shape your own reality.

You are part of a universal energy of life called Infinite Intelligence. You are, therefore, not separate from any other human being. Fear is an illusion that stems from a sense of separation. Your anger alerts you to this illusion of separation that you need to heal.

5

WHY EVERY THOUGHT AND BELIEF IS A PRAYER

If you are a part of one creative ocean of intelligent energy, then the most logical conclusion is that every single thought you have is a prayer; when you engage in thoughts, words, and actions, they "come back" as experience. This is the law of cause and effect. Your entire life right now (the effect) has happened because of all the choices or thoughts that you made in the past (cause). Before you bring anything into physical reality it must have been preceded by thought. There are two very important implications of the power of your thoughts to affect your reality:

1. **Every thought you have has a physical impact on your health.** We discussed in Chapter 2 that anger is related to a host of diseases. The reason for this is that anger is associated with negative thoughts, which are responsible for weakening your immune system and causing the body to release harmful chemicals. The relatively new field of psychoneuroimmunology (PNI) research has supported the view that the mind and immune system are not separate and actually work together. This implies that your mind simply is not lodged in your brain, but is all over your body.

2. **Your thoughts affect your perceived "outer" world of relationships, finances, career, and so forth.** The reason for this is that according to quantum physics and Ayurveda, the Universe is an extension of you.

Your thoughts, both conscious and subconscious, are the creative force with which Infinite Intelligence expresses itself through you. This means that all the thoughts that you have will materialize to form your own reality. In this sense, every thought is a prayer, because you are getting whatever you are asking for.

Your thoughts also consist of subconscious thoughts that you are not aware of. Subconscious thoughts are beliefs that you hold about yourself and about life in general that are below the surface of your conscious thoughts. Subconscious thoughts are ideas that you hold to be true. We will show in Chapter 17 that your beliefs can have a powerful effect on you through the placebo effect.

These beliefs are the ones that have been programmed into you by your parents, teachers, and environment; for example, consciously you might think, "I would like this thing," but subconsciously you might believe, "I don't deserve this." Or, you may think, "I would like to write a book," but subconsciously you may believe, "I am not capable of doing it."

As you saw in Figure 2 in Chapter 4, your mind, which generates thought, is linked to the quantum energy field where ideas crystallize and waves and particles begin the process of taking form. From the analogy that was described earlier, you can view each thought as a brush stroke, which combine together to create a picture of your life.

All the individual brushstrokes can create a very beautiful picture or they can create an ugly one. Similarly, if you think angry, critical, or judgmental thoughts, then that is what will show up in your life; also, if you have conscious, loving thoughts on the surface, but your beliefs are based on resentment and fear, the net impact may be an angry or fearful reality, depending on how strong the pull of your subconscious beliefs are.

You may go to church for an hour to attend Sunday mass and have peaceful, conscious thoughts during that time; however, if during the rest of the week you have conscious thoughts that are based on stress, anger, and unresolved negative subconscious beliefs, the pull of your reality will be towards what you are thinking and believing most of the time (i.e., a stressful and angry reality). On the other hand, if your thoughts are based on peace and are stronger than any negative subconscious thoughts such as resentment, this will, in general, create a peaceful reality.

As human beings we have the ability to choose our thoughts, including the ones we are not aware of. The problem, however, is that many of us do not exercise that choice because we simply do not know how. As we will present in Part II, our anger can alert us to some of the subconscious illusions of separation that we may have. If we are willing to listen to these alerts, we can actually transform our anger and allow it to lead us to our divinity, which is love.

If we become more aware of how and what we think consistently and change our subconscious beliefs, we can recognize our true divine being and lead a glorious and abundant life. Living in this state is the most natural state of being and is our birthright. On the other hand, if we do not listen to our anger alerts, this can lead to more emotional pain.

Our thoughts and beliefs have a direct effect on our bodies and create the life that we experience.

6

THE MIRROR OF LIFE: WHY ANGER GENERATES ANGER

*T*he life that you experience is like one big mirror that reflects you. The people in your life, as well as the situations and events that happen, are life reflecting back to you the thoughts and beliefs you have about yourself. The last chapter provided the logic why this is so. To recap very briefly: Your thoughts are the "tools" through which Infinite Intelligence uses to express itself in the physical world; thoughts, which come from the quantum realm, are the creative force of the Divine. You, who are divine by nature, therefore "create" your life with your thoughts.

Your thoughts, words, and actions end up materializing your experience of life. This happens irrespective of whether the thoughts are "good" or "bad." In other words, what you send out comes back to you. This means that angry thoughts, words, and actions that are hurtful can come back to haunt you.

We would like to stress one point: Even if you have been reactive and hurtful, **but have made a sincere effort to understand the lesson behind the angry event, forgiven, or have sought forgiveness, the boomerang impact of your negative energy will be muted, or it may completely dissipate.** Infinite Intelligence always acknowledges your willingness to make changes in your life, no matter how small it is. This is known as grace.

Because so many of us are not aware of our true reality as divine beings, we feel that life is based on the random flow of events and that we have little influence on creating our destiny. We assume that our thoughts, words, and actions are somehow not connected to the events and situations that happen in our life, as well as the people who show up in our life. There are no "accidents" in this world because life is one, and we as human beings are a part of it.

We would like to give you two real stories of how anger, when reactively expressed in a hurtful way and when it was pent-up as resentment, literally "came back" as experience. The purpose of this section is to show you how you can generate more emotional pain in your life if you do not know how the Universe operates from a spiritual standpoint.

Aside from the possibility of creating physical disease, anger can cause us increasing levels of emotional pain if we are not willing to learn from it. All names and identifying details have been changed beyond recognition to protect the privacy of individuals.

THE CASE OF ANGRY ANDREW

Andrew worked for a company where he had developed a reputation for being highly competent. He had been married to Judy, a housewife, for many years. Professionally, his dream was to become the head of his department whereby he would continue to make significant contributions to his field. While Andrew was generally a kind person at heart, he had a big ego and expressed his anger quite reactively, especially to Judy.

The day came when finally he became the head of his department. His ego became more inflated, and he became more reactive and verbally abusive towards Judy. Although they had been married for many years, she never felt so emotionally isolated from her husband. Andrew shouted at the top of his voice often and was not able to verbally express his thoughts and feelings in a responsible way.

Shortly after this round of angry verbal abuse, an amazing set of events happened in his professional life, which involved angering Andrew's superiors. These events led to Andrew's dismissal from his position as the department head. In the history of the company this was the first time something like this had happened. From a spiritual standpoint Andrew was "isolated" from his job. In other words, his angry words literally "came back" and materialized as experience.

Soon after this event, Andrew suffered from a heart attack and then a stroke, symbolizing his lack of love for himself and his sense of isolation from others, including his wife. The sad part of this story is that Andrew never saw the spiritual connection between the angry words in his personal life and the events that happened in his professional life.

THE CASE OF RESENTFUL ROBERTA

Roberta finished her medical training and joined a physician group practice. Her new employers were also friends of her uncle who was a well-known physician in a local hospital. Roberta thought she was offered a decent compensation package. She, however, did not think it was necessary to have some of the conditions of her employment written in her contract. In particular, she verbally accepted from her employers that within 3 years she would be given a partnership in the practice. She simply "trusted" her employers.

After a while on the job, she discovered that she was being paid less than the market rate. Further, 3 years went by, and there was no offer of partnership from her employers. When she approached them about the partnership, she was told that she "was not generating enough revenue" for the practice, and would have to wait 2 more years. Roberta felt very angry about the situation. Thoughts such as the following raced through her mind: "I feel cheated. I have worked so hard and this is what I get in return? They have been using me." Roberta did not express these feelings to her employers.

With enormous resentment inside her, she notified her present employers that she was going to join another practice in a neighboring state. Her ultimate intention was to leave the current job and find "greener pastures." Her current employers felt obliged to keep her position because they wanted to maintain connections with Roberta's politically influential uncle.

After joining her new practice, Roberta was disappointed to find that her new employers treated her worse than her previous employers. She notified her previous employers that she wanted to come back. While the previous employers allowed her to come back, they offered her a new contract, which required her to stay in the practice for another 3 years before allowing partnership in the practice.

It was a "take it or leave it" deal with no scope for negotiation. Roberta became even more resentful. She did not realize, however, that her resentment kept on breeding more resentful situations. Instead of taking responsibility, she blamed her employers for her experience.

In both the cases of Andrew and Roberta, the feelings of anger per se were not the problem. The issue was what they said or did with that anger. In Andrew's case, he reactively expressed his anger and in Roberta's case, she suppressed it. Neither of them was aware of the spiritual significance of their anger and did not have the knowledge of how to express it in a healthy way. If Andrew was able to realize the spiritual importance of his anger, it is unlikely that the boomerang impact of his words would have come back, as the Universe is full of mercy.

The reason why our pain escalates often is that we do not listen to the messages of our feelings before there is a crisis. Too frequently, it takes a crisis to "wake us up" to our true spiritual reality. Life, however, does not have to be full of crises. If we listen to the messages of our anger, and think and act in a healthy way, we can be assured of smooth sailing.

How Anger Is Mirrored from Generation to Generation

There are two ways anger can be passed on from one generation to another. One way is the emotional pain our parents or caregivers may have inflicted on us when we were young. We may have anger toward them that is buried within us. Another way anger is passed on is the way we express our anger. If we are habitually reactive, these patterns may have developed from our parents and those who brought us up. Some of these habits have been programmed into us when we were little children. Because of this, many of us are not even aware that these habits came from our caregivers.

If you saw your parents express anger in hurtful ways, maybe you also learned to express anger in the same way as your parents did. You may not even be aware that you lash out with hurtful words without pausing when you are angry. Saying things without pausing and thinking through the issues when you are angry is known as being reactive. On the other hand, you may have been taught during childhood that it was not acceptable to express anger at all. As an adult, therefore, you may not express your anger and keep it inside instead.

Reactive behavior is often based on subconscious beliefs about how to express anger. As we mentioned in Chapter 5 on "Why Every Thought Is a Prayer," our subconscious thoughts are the ones that we may not always be aware of. A lack of awareness of our subconscious thoughts often leads us to be reactive. In Part III, we will discuss how to pause, step back from our anger, and allow ourselves to learn from it.

Many of us are caught up in vicious cycles of unhealthy habits, which are passed on from generation to generation. We need to pause, step back, and learn to get out of these vicious cycles. Instead of blaming our parents, the spiritual test is to express and communicate our anger in a healthy way without being reactive and to learn its spiritual lessons. Parts II and III will show you how to manage and communicate your anger wisely and how you can learn about yourself from such experiences.

Be careful of what you think and say when you are angry— angry thoughts may boomerang back to you. Resentful thoughts create resentful experiences. We learn how to express our anger from our caregivers. The spiritual test is to manage and express our anger wisely, as well as to learn and reflect on the areas where we need to heal.

$\mathscr{P}$ART II

How to Use Anger as a Pathway to Find Healing and Love

7

ANGER AS A PATHWAY TO RESPONSIBILITY

*A*s we saw in Part I, we can go round and round in the vicious cycles of anger within our own life and from one generation to another. Along the way, our anger can make us fall prey to disease and premature death. How do we break away from such cycles and instead use the energy of anger to lead us to peace and happiness? This chapter, along with the forthcoming ones in Part II, will give you the spiritual understanding that is necessary for you to break away from such vicious cycles, so that you may use your anger as a pathway to healing and love.

Angry experiences in your outer life are a reflection of inner conflict, as life simply mirrors the inner spaces that need to heal. Anger, therefore, alerts you that you need to do spiritual work on yourself. This chapter shows you how anger can alert you of the need to become responsible and why this is an important aspect of love that needs to be learned.

Without personal responsibility for the affairs of your life, it is virtually impossible to succeed in any major area of your life. Although you may have legitimate concerns in your life, the important point, however, is your ability to respond to such concerns and your decision to learn from them. From a spiritual sense, a "problem" really does not exist. It is how you interpret and label the "problem."

If you label your concern as a problem in your mind, then it is likely that you will face anger. The message of your anger is that you need to change your label of "problem" into a label of "learning." If you are able to do this, this will solve 99 percent of your emotional pain. Often it is too difficult for us to accept personal responsibility because we think we are separate from each other and are not connected.

If you face a situation or person that angers you, the foremost question that you need to ask yourself is, "How have I contributed to or created this situation?" Is it some past thought, word, or action that is "coming back" to me now? If you can see the connection between past action and what is happening now, it is important to acknowledge that and say, "Yes, I did that." The latter statement simply affirms that you believe you are a cocreator of your life and believe in the law of cause and effect. This is one meaning of responsibility.

Another meaning of responsibility is the "ability to respond." Before you respond to a stimulus (e.g., an outside event or something someone said to you), there is a gap between the stimulus and your response. It is within this space that you have the opportunity to *think and choose* your response instead of automatically doing what you have been doing all along (i.e., being reactive).

An example of a reactive response is, "I don't understand why he did this to me." The more conscious you are about your thoughts, the more you will be able to choose a creative response. In other words, you will be less reactive and instead be more proactive. **It is not what happens to you, it is how you choose to think about what happens to you.**

In Chapter 18, we will discuss in detail how to become more responsible through meditation. Being responsible means that you should be able to step back and pause for any situation where you have angry feelings. If you can step back and pause, you will be able to proactively think about how you are going to respond. Secondly, you will be able to reflect why you may have attracted such a situation in your life and learn from that experience.

The opposite of responsibility is blame. As we said in Chapter 6, there is no such thing as "blame" from a spiritual standpoint. The anger that you face when you blame someone or some event is an indication that you need to release blame. If things are not going right for some reason, think of all the things or persons who are on your blame "hit" list: your parents, your lover, your children, your boss, your neighbors, the economy, the weather, the political climate, and so on.

In fact, you can truly make up an infinite list of people, things, or events that are "causing" your negative situation. Instead of thinking, "This happened to me because he/she did it," the more responsible way to think is, "I am here today because of all the choices I made in the past. I will learn from this situation and move on."

In the case of "Resentful Roberta" in Chapter 6, we saw that Roberta was unable to take responsibility and learn from her experiences. She frequently complained and blamed her employers for her situation. Instead of feeling angry and cheated, a more responsible approach would have been to acknowledge that she did not negotiate her compensation package in writing and that she would make sure something similar did not happen in the future.

Because Roberta was unable to find the spiritual meaning of her anger, she was unknowingly creating more resentful situations. Resentful patterns kept on being repeated because the Universe was trying to teach her to be responsible. Sometimes the events in our lives tend to get "worse" from our human perspective; however, it is God's way of ringing the bell louder, so that we listen and hear the messages of our angry feelings with more attention.

Life, including us, is one conscious sea of energy. It does not make any logical or spiritual sense to point a finger at anyone implicating them for blame, because "we" are "them" from an energy standpoint. This is a scientific fact. We are cocreators of our lives because every conscious and unconscious thought materializes as experience through quantum reality. We may deny responsibility, but the truth is we are creating our own lives moment by moment through our own thoughts, words, and actions.

The biggest barrier to being responsible is that you may not be aware of your conscious and subconscious thoughts and the role they have in creating your reality. You may believe that your thoughts and beliefs have no influence on shaping your life. As we have said before, this is not so. Refer back to Chapter 4 and refresh your memory regarding why this is not true. Becoming aware of what you think and believe is the spiritual challenge.

In order to help you understand how accepting more personal responsibility in your life will literally change your life for the better, let me (Reshmi) illustrate with an example from my own life how anger taught me about personal responsibility. When my daughter, Rania, was 3 years old, there were many instances when she aroused anger in me. I often responded reactively, for example, when she spilled milk on the table.

These situations were compounded by the fact that she was having mini-fights with her little brother. I was getting quite distressed, and I wondered how I could better manage such situations. I also wondered why Rania was responding to simple, even-toned requests in a rebellious way.

After much reflection and spiritual reading, it dawned on me that I was responsible for creating these events at home. I realized that my own thoughts and words were literally "coming back to me." As you will recall from Chapters 4 and 5, our thoughts are creative energy, which have a power of their own. Further, they are always reflected back to us as experiences, just as a mirror reflects light. My daughter was simply reflecting back the negative energy that I was giving out. I clearly acknowledged to myself that I was the "cause" of my negative experiences.

Determined to change the situation in my home life, I responded to future liquid spills calmly with, "Let us clean it up,

Rania. Don't worry about it, it is only a spill." Initially, the angry energy still passed through me, but I stepped back each time and paused before giving any answer. **Over time, however, these situations no longer aroused angry feelings anymore. It appeared that these angry feelings had fulfilled their purpose in teaching me about responsibility.**

I also realized I had some buried resentment from past experiences. The pent-up resentment I had toward various people was manifesting as displaced anger toward my daughter. I tried to think about any resentful situations I had in the past and released these blocked emotions through a process of forgiveness. In Part III, you will see that forgiveness is a very important part of anger management; you will also learn the necessary steps for forgiveness.

Shortly after my resolve to change how I was going to respond to my children, along with giving Rania more loving attention (as described in "Managing Anger in Children" in Chapter 19), I began to see little miracles pop up at home and in other areas of my life. At home, Rania stopped responding in an angry and loud voice to simple requests. She also fought less with her little brother.

More amazingly, though, I was able to see a difference in my relationships outside my home-life. I came across people who were calmer, less critical, and less annoyed in virtually all areas of my life, whether it was cab drivers, store clerks, or acquaintances. This was proof to me that my thoughts shaped my experiences of life by attracting people who mirrored the new me. It also illustrated to me that when we change our thoughts and beliefs, our new way of thinking will repel people who do not reflect our new beliefs. It proved to me beyond doubt that life is not based on random events and "accidents," but is a part of one connected whole.

Being reactive when you become angry means that you are not aware of your thoughts and that you are, in effect, trapped by past memories. The best analogy of this is like a dog that starts salivating with the tinkling of a bell, whether there is food or no food. The dog's association of food with a bell from past memory automatically causes it to salivate now. This also is how you behave when you become reactive in a situation that arouses anger. Once you are aware of what you think and believe, your ability to respond also increases; i.e., you become responsible.

How do you become more aware of your thoughts and beliefs? The best way to do this is through meditation which we will discuss in Part III. Meditation will enable you to pause and step back. Pausing and stepping back is the same thing as observing your thoughts. If you recall, Figure 2 in Chapter 4 shows that you are made of three layers: soul, mind, and body. To observe your thoughts you have to step out of your mind and view it from the position of the soul. When you view your life and events from the perspective of the soul, you essentially become an observer of your life.

By being an observer, just like seeing a movie, you can become detached from the events. Once you become detached, you can say to yourself, "This is only the movie of life, no big deal." It is like taking a 30,000 aerial foot view and seeing the angry event as a speck that has no significance at all. To become an observer, you have to get in touch with your soul every day, or at least on a regular basis. We will discuss this in more detail in Chapter 18 in the section on "Meditation: Learning to Pause and Step Back."

In addition to meditation, you may also want to catch yourself when you speak in reactive phrases and words. What you speak is a good indication of what you think and believe. For example, change:

- "I have to do this," to "I **choose** to do this."
- "I don't have much choice," to "I have **unlimited choices** in my life."

- "I don't have any control over the situation," to "I have **control over how I think** about the situation."
- "I won't be allowed to do that," to "Let me **explore the alternatives.**"

In summary, therefore, learn to **pause, think,** and then **choose** your response. Meditation will help you learn to pause. Think about the situation and try to see how the law of cause and effect is playing out in your life. Decide how you will respond and imagine what the consequences would be if you made that choice. Choose a response that will be beneficial to you and others. How do you know you have made a right choice? Your choice is right when you get a pleasant feeling associated with it.

The process of becoming responsible is also a process of realizing that you are a divine being. It means removing one by one all the illusions of limitations that you may have. In the next chapter we will discuss how anger may help you to release negative perceptions about yourself.

Anger can help us to become more responsible. Once we have learned the ability to respond to any situation in a healthy way, events that generate anger will disappear from our lives.

8

ANGER AS A PATHWAY TO SELF-ESTEEM

*S*elf-esteem simply refers to how much you like yourself. The sad truth is that there is a worldwide epidemic of low self-esteem based on the belief that we are physically separate and small. As we noted in Part I, nothing could be further from the truth. Modern telescopes and satellites have confirmed that the Universe is composed of 99 percent invisible energy and less than 1 percent matter; further, 1 percent matter is also energy when seen through super magnified lens.

The most logical conclusion then is that you too are an invisible being having a temporary material existence. However, most of us have it the other way around: We believe that our material existence is primary and our spiritual experience is secondary. The truth is that our human eyes are not capable of seeing the vast swirl of energies contained in so-called "solid" objects. Because we only "see" our physical bodies, we believe that we are separate and not connected.

If you believe that you are small and separate from everyone else, your thoughts and internal belief patterns may be along the following lines:

- I don't count in the scheme of things.
- I don't appreciate myself.
- My situation is hopeless.

- I don't deserve the best in life.
- I don't like myself deep down.
- I could never be a success.
- She/he is more talented than I am.

The Universe is evolutionary in nature. The natural force in the Universe is towards growth and maturity. In this scheme of things, the Universe would also like your thinking to mature so that you realize that you are an infinite being; at some point in your life, therefore, you will be forced to deal head-on with the mistaken belief of separation and the associated belief patterns of low self-esteem. One way to do this is to convince your mind with the scientific knowledge that you are not separate from Infinite Intelligence.

In fact, our discussion on quantum physics in Chapter 4 was done with the intention of persuading your mind to believe that you are part of one, divine energy. Your ego believes in things that it only sees. Your job is to convince your ego that just because it does not see the vast oneness of energy that does not necessarily mean it is does not exist. You don't have to physically see to believe. Every material object, including your body, is condensed energy.

For many people, however, the method of gaining knowledge of their divinity through scientific information may be hard to understand; this is a method they may have never come across. For those people who can't learn or are not familiar with this method, the Universe will teach them through a method of actual life experiences, which can also be emotionally painful. This is the hard way. The hard way involves being taken advantage of or being a victim in some way. In fact, most people are taught this way. The anger that they feel when they are a victim is simply a message that they need to love themselves more and realize that they are divine.

Loving yourself means realizing that you are one with everyone. It should not be confused with the ego belief that you are superior to anyone else. In practical terms, loving yourself means that you deserve the very best that life has to offer both physically and emotionally. It means that you should not tolerate your own inner dialogue of criticism. It also implies that you may need to garner the courage to speak up when you have to. After taking corrective action to restore your self-esteem, the second step is to nurture it on a regular basis, so it continues to grow.

You become a victim when you give your power away to others. This happens because of your beliefs of low self-esteem, which in turn is based on an illusion of separation from your ultimate source of Infinite Intelligence. We can draw an analogy of a drop of water that feels that it does not belong to the ocean. The drop of water mistakenly believes that it is not made of the same substance as the ocean.

If you become victimized and are angry about it, then you have to ask yourself what mistaken belief patterns you are still holding on to. Your anger is simply sending the message that "something is not right." It is up to you to figure out what is not right in your belief pattern.

In fact, the angrier you are, the more likely it is that you have certain belief patterns of low self-esteem that are deeply embedded in your subconscious. Your task is to change these beliefs of unworthiness to beliefs of infinite potential. You might not understand the lesson the first time around. You may even need repeated lessons of victimization and anger until you get the message. It could take a momentary flash of insight to understand and change your beliefs. Or it could take even a lifetime. It will depend on where you are on the path of your spiritual evolution.

An example of where anger can lead the victim within us to become victorious is an experience we had with an ex-accountant of ours a few years ago. We asked our accountant named David (not his real name) to prepare our annual tax returns. As mutually agreed upon, David was going to bill us for the amount of time that he took to do our returns. We called around to get a few other estimates and found out that the cost of tax preparation would be in the range of $250 to $300. This is also what we expected from David, although we did not explicitly discuss this with him.

As it turned out, not only did David do a sloppy job by making mistakes in his calculations, he sent us a bill for $700! Obviously we were both shocked and angry, as we felt he was taking advantage of us. We clearly decided that we were not going to pay this amount. We were also concerned that if we did not act, he would take advantage of other people, too.

As both of us were not in the mood to confront the accountant directly, we decided to write a letter. The letter was very polite and expressed our anger in a diplomatic way. There were three elements to this letter: (a) The first paragraph *praised* him for his services; (b) the second paragraph expressed our *concerns* that his price was almost double the market rate, especially given the mistakes he had made in the calculations; and (c) the last paragraph asked him to *consider* lowering his fees in line with the market rate.

After a couple of days, we called him and asked him if he had received the letter. He said he had. Further, on his own account he said he would lower his fees to what we requested. There was no confrontation and the issue was resolved peacefully. In Chapter 19 we will discuss in detail how to express angry feelings in a peaceful way without causing resentment or anger in others.

As another example, let us discuss the case of Judy, the wife of "Angry Andrew" in Chapter 6. Judy's example will make you aware of negative self-esteem patterns and how they manifest as victim situations. As you will recall, Judy was a wife who suffered verbal abuse from her husband.

This abuse not only hurt Judy, but also made her angry. After much reflection, it finally dawned on her that she was responsible for allowing her husband to take her for granted. Rarely was she able to garner the courage to speak up and defend herself. In other words, she had suppressed anger, which was turning into depression.

Making matters worse, she realized that she had not asserted her rights, especially in financial matters. She realized that there was a direct relationship between her economic dependence on her husband and the level of his verbal abuse. As she found out later, their vacation home was solely in her husband's name, as were most of their stock investments. She realized that she had not taken financial responsibility in these matters and should have done so.

Judy had many opportunities in the past to seek further education and get more financial skills, but never bothered to do so. As with so many women, Judy's beliefs of low self-esteem and self-sabotage were along the lines of, "I don't think I have the brains for further education;" "I don't need a better education for myself because my husband will support me;" "My main function in life is a caregiver of my children;" "My partner is much smarter than I am;" "My partner has all the degrees, so he is more capable of making the right decisions for our family."

The beliefs just described are common among many women. If you have been victimized in a relationship, take a close inner look to see if you have any of these patterns of belief. One way to determine this is to see what words come out of your mouth during a conversation. If you say anything about yourself that implies inferiority, this means that you have low self-esteem beliefs. If you do, change the negative belief into a positive statement to repeat several times, many times a day, over a course of a few weeks. Doing so will allow the new belief to get ingrained into your subconscious. Here are some examples of some positive belief statements:

- I am a highly intelligent person with infinite potential.
- I deserve the best life has to offer.
- I can achieve anything in life that I want.
- I am a loving person.

• I am a successful person.
• I have great health.
• I am a patient parent.

The previous list gives examples of affirmations, which are essentially positive statements about yourself. As we shall show you in Part III, they *do* work, and there is scientific evidence to back it up.

Let us go back to Judy now. While Judy considered separation, she also realized that she was attached to the material comfort and financial security of the marriage. Being a homemaker during her entire marriage, the thought of taking care of herself physically frightened her. Judy eventually did stay in the marriage despite the fact that it was an unsatisfactory situation.

In addition to her anger, Judy was also very fearful of losing what she already had. In fact, anger and fear often go hand in hand. Although anger may indicate that we need to take action to stop being victims, many of us are too scared to do so. Many of us would rather remain victims in abusive relationships than lose our material comforts. In other words, we often compromise our spiritual growth for material security. Our fear arises because we do not trust God enough to take care of our emotional, spiritual, and physical needs; however, as we noted in Chapter 4, fear is only an illusion. It is based on the false belief that we are all separate.

We are, in fact, part of the divine energy that is universal. What is there to fear if God is always with us? Once we cultivate a sense of trust within us that we are divine, all our needs will be taken care of automatically, whatever they may be. When we remove fear with love, miracles can happen. We have seen this happen in our own lives and testify that this is true. Trusting more of our intuition and feelings means trusting more of God. When we do this, we will see that life will unfold in beautiful and fulfilling ways.

The process of gaining self-esteem and realizing your divine potential is not something that simply happens by changing a few beliefs. It means changing a host of beliefs that you may be addicted to. At a conscious level you may not realize that you have such addictions. The purpose of the next chapter is to show how anger can help you reveal some of these inner attachments.

Our self-esteem is the center of our soul. The anger that we experience may indicate that we need to honor and nourish our self-esteem, so that we develop authentic power. Often our anger implies that we need to rightfully reclaim any power we have given away.

9

ANGER AS A PATHWAY TO FREEDOM FROM INNER ADDICTIONS

*O*ften we are attached to certain attitudes, beliefs, or things in life. When we lose these attachments or addictions, we may feel anger. Anger, then, is pointing us to our attachments that we need to let go of. We cannot make room for our divinity if our inner space is filled with the clutter of thoughts and beliefs that make us feel separate from other human beings and from our source of Infinite Intelligence.

Many people have physical addictions such as alcohol or drugs. For the vast majority of us, though, our addictions are attachments of our minds. The word "addiction," therefore, is used in the broadest sense of the term. We could be attached to our job, money, position in society, security, or comfort. We could also be attached to our nationality. Our addiction could be our family or perhaps tribal beliefs that no longer serve us.

The anger that we feel when we lose these intangible things may indicate that we need to examine what we are attached to and that maybe it is time to let go of those attachments. If, for example, you lost a promotion to a rival coworker, the anger you may feel because you were overlooked might indicate that you are too attached to your job.

Following is a checklist of some common intangible addictions that you may need to release if anger is the symptom that you are experiencing. Look at the categories and ask yourself if you are attached to any of them.

- *Security.* This refers to a sense that everything will continue to be the way it has been. Our sense of security could be shaken if we lose a loved one or if we lose our jobs due to an economic downturn, for example. Our true sense of security, however, comes not by assuming that the outer world will not change, but by a realization that our soul does not change. Change and decay are a constant in the material world and this is something that we have to learn to accept.
- *Safety.* We may feel violated if we have been harmed physically or emotionally. A sense of vulnerability to harm, however, occurs if we live in fear. Fear, in turn, stems from a sense that we are all separate. When we realize the same divine presence permeating through each and every human being, we then realize that fear is only a false illusion in our own minds. A true sense of safety can only come about if we release the false illusion of fear in our minds and fill the gap with the realization that we are One Love.
- *Nationality or Race.* We may be attached to a sense of pride that occurs when we think that our own nation or race is superior to other nations and races. As we saw in Chapter 4, this does not make any logical sense whatsoever from a spiritual standpoint. Literally, we are one and interconnected. It behooves each one of us to think beyond artificial political boundaries by thinking universally.
- *Religion.* If you have been born into a formal religion, how often have you thought that your religion was "right" and theirs was "wrong?" This kind of thinking, as you see, automatically causes separation. At a superficial level, there may appear to be differences. However, the deeper we go into each of the major religions in the world, we realize there are no differences. Whether we call Infinite Intelligence by the name of God, Allah, Yahweh, or Brahma, it does not matter. One can draw an analogy of climbing a mountain (to reach

the peak of Love). It does not matter from which side you climb the mountain because you are on the same mountain, trying to reach the same peak.

- *Power and Status.* The power and status that we normally think of refers to external power, as in our occupations or the titles associated with our jobs. Power and status could also come from our material wealth, which might lead us to feel superior or inferior to other human beings. There is nothing wrong per se in seeking greater external power and wealth. The problem arises when we do so in a mindless game whereby those pursuits become ends in themselves, rather than a means to further nourish our souls.

As we noted in the introduction of this book, whenever God wants to communicate with us, He often does so through symbolic events. In order to help you understand how God might be sending a message for you to release your attachments, let me (Reshmi) tell you a story of how I released some of my own attachments through anger. This story will also help you understand how divine messages are communicated through symbolic language.

The incident happened one summer evening when we were having a barbeque party. A number of people had been invited. They were enjoying their meal, both inside the house as well as outside on the porch. As a host, I was going around talking to my guests. As I entered one section of the living room, I realized in horror that there was a big ketchup stain on my light beige carpet. Apparently someone had spilled the ketchup and had tried to clean it off. I could literally feel a strong current of anger pass through me as I examined the carpet further. What angered me more was that the "culprit" did not reveal him or herself. As a host, I could not say anything or show my displeasure.

As I tried to clean up the spill, the stain got even more ingrained into the carpet. Feeling very angry about the situation, my entire evening was ruined. I thought about the expense of professional cleaning and the need for possibly replacing the carpet altogether.

Later that evening after the guests had left, I began to reflect on the incident in a cooler headed manner. What was the meaning of all this? What did the "stain" really represent? How was I responsible for this, and what did this teach me about myself? The answers became clear while I began to read through Louise Hay's book, *The Power Is Within You.* I came across the word "stain" on page 7 of the book: "As you repeat thoughts over and over, you first notice a stain on the carpet. . . ."

In fact, since the last few weeks, I had been absorbed by negative thoughts about someone whom I thought had "wronged me." I realized that I was holding on to those memories too long. In other words, my attachment to the negative memories of a past experience was a "stain" on the screen of my mind. I also realized that I was attached to the obsessive spotless cleanliness of my carpet. That also represented a "stain." I understood that I needed to let go of my attachment there as well. All material things will eventually decay, so why was I attached to it so much?

Since the Universe is always trying to assess whether we have learned our lessons, it brings more spiritual tests. Every lesson that we get is simply another way of exposing one more layer of our soul and divinity. Indeed, the next evening my son smeared a lot of toothpaste onto one section of the carpet. Once again I was irritated, but this time I did not feel the intense anger I felt the previous night. I took a deep breath and cleaned the mess up.

This example illustrates how anger can alert you of your false attachments. Often we get angry when we lose the things that we are attached or addicted to. In my case, I "lost" my carpet. This was a bigger reflection of my attachment to material comforts. Any loss we experience and the anger that is associated with it is a message from the Universe to look within ourselves.

Since we always feel a gap when we lose an attachment or addiction, God is asking us indirectly to fill the empty space with Him. God says to us during these times, "Let go of your false illusion, and look at the true divine nature of your own Being." God wants to convey to us that whatever we want in life to make us truly fulfilled is already within us. We do not need to look for it outside of ourselves.

Since many of the attachments in our lives are part of our subconscious beings, we may not be aware of them; however, in Chapter 5 on "Why Every Thought and Belief Is a Prayer," we saw that our subconscious beliefs are mirrored in the life that we experience. Angry situations actually give us an opportunity to do some serious reflection and help us to see what attachments we need to release at the subconscious level.

Unless we are able to acknowledge and release those false attachments, the Universe will repeatedly bring us angry experiences in various forms and disguises. Because God loves us so much, every angry and painful experience is really a blessing in disguise. It is a blessing because we are given the opportunity to bring forth the True Light within ourselves.

Anger can guide us to recognize the false attachments and addictions we cling to. It may indicate that we need to let go of these attachments. When we are free of our false attachments, we are free to experience our true divinity.

10

ANGER AS A PATHWAY TO PROSPERITY

*Y*ou may not realize it, but the extent of true prosperity in your life is directly related to the extent of your self-esteem and the extent you have removed false inner addictions from your life. The more you are aware that you are a divine being with infinite potential, the more prosperous you are likely to be. In other words, prosperity is about your state of mind, both at conscious and subconscious levels. If you, therefore, thought that prosperity had to do with money only, think again.

Money is an important component of prosperity, but there are other components such as loving relationships, sufficient leisure time, comfort, good health, a creative outlet for your talents, and the ability to sleep at night with peace of mind. By this definition, how many of these components of prosperity do you have? If you have all of these, you are a very fortunate person.

In recent years, we have faced an economy of high unemployment, stock market losses, and corporate scandals of greed. Many of us have been affected either directly or indirectly by these events. These events have also generated anger and anxiety. One major health symptom of these emotional pains is that a lot of us can't sleep well at night, as confirmed by recent national health surveys. In fact, if you are unable to sleep at night due to anger and anxiety about financial issues, your lack of sleep can be literally life-threatening and pose significant health hazards. As shown in Chapter 2, there is scientific medical evidence that inability to sleep is related to a host of health problems such as heart disease, infections, accidents, and sexual dysfunction.[1]

Let us stress that your inability to sleep due to anger and anxiety can end up being a vicious cycle, which ultimately takes you even further away from your goals of prosperity. A 1-hour sleep loss every night for an entire week is the same as being without sleep an entire night. Further, you can't repay this sleep debt by one night of good sleep. It may take several weeks, just like it may take several weeks to reduce your weight on a diet program.

As you incur more and more sleep debt due to your original anger and anxiety, you will find that you will become more irritable and angry during the day because of your inability to cope with simple workloads. You will also find that you have reduced productivity due to your inability to think logically, remember things, handle complex tasks, and analyze new information. It also means that you will be less creative.

Your productivity is directly related to how much wealth you create in your life. The bottom line is this: Mismanagement of your anger and anxiety will lead to a downward spiral of worsening sleep, productivity, and general health. In other words, this chain of events will have a big impact on your overall prosperity.

If you are angry and frustrated because of your inability to become financially independent, or because of a job loss, or because of an argument with your spouse, the first thing you need to become aware of is your limited beliefs on prosperity. Your anger is simply alerting you that you need to release these beliefs.

---

[1]Please visit our Web site, www.SleepHealthDoc.com, to get your free special report on how to get quality sleep for good health.

Your beliefs on money and prosperity were formed in child-hood, most likely from your parents and caregivers and your environment. Here are some common limiting beliefs:

- I have to work hard to earn a living.
- I never make ends meet.
- Stock brokers are dishonest.
- I'm sick and tired of my bills.
- I am not worthy of the best.
- I never have enough time.
- I am envious of people who have more than me.
- My needs come last in the family.
- I'll take care of my health later.
- I'll skimp on my sleep because I have too much to do.

Which of these beliefs do you hold? Do some reflection and think about it. Also be conscious of what you say, as your words will give you an idea of what your thoughts and beliefs are. Just remember, the ancestor to every word is a thought. You could not have said something unless you thought about it or believed it.

The reason why all these beliefs are limiting is because they are based on the assumption that there is not enough in the Universe. These are all ego beliefs of scarcity. Remember the corollary: If you believe in scarcity, then that is what you will get in life. Your thoughts and subconscious beliefs create experience.

Once again, we want to remind you that these scarcity ego beliefs don't make logical sense. You are part of the Infinite. There is, therefore, no need to believe in scarcity. It is like imagining that you have access to a huge infinite ocean. No matter how much you take from it, its supply will never be diminished and there will always be enough for everyone.

If your thoughts are based on poverty, it is like taking a small cup from this ocean and looking at it and saying to yourself that there is never enough. In fact, the more poverty conscious beliefs you hold onto, the more likely you will face anger in situations dealing with financial issues. The anger is there to help you realize that you need to change your poverty beliefs into abundant beliefs.

How do you go about changing poverty beliefs into prosperity beliefs? One way to do this is to use repeated affirmations or positive self-talk on prosperity. For example, take one of the beliefs in the previous list such as, "I am not worthy," and change it to, "**I deserve the best in life.**" Repeat this a couple of times a day for several weeks until you really believe it.

Some of the wealthiest men in the last 100 years such as Andrew Carnegie and Henry Ford followed this practice of wealth affirmation to make them financially rich. This was outlined by Naploean Hill in his book, *Think and Grow Rich.* Napoleon Hill was commissioned by Andrew Carnegie to do a study of the factors that made ordinary men very wealthy. One of the factors for their success was the practice of daily affirmations (or *autosuggestions,* a term used by Napoleon Hill).

The big test of your belief in these new affirmations is whether you can truly be generous at a practical level. If you want love in your life, you must give love. If you want friendship, you must be a friend. If you want more money in your life, you must give some money away. You will find that some of the wealthiest families in America practice tithing, which is giving 10 percent of their income away for charitable purposes. Furthermore, many of them started this practice even when they were poor. It is not something they did once they could afford it.

If you are worried and angry about a prosperity issue, start giving away some of what you are concerned about. If you are concerned about money, for example, then give away money on a regular basis, even if it is $1 a month. This process will set in motion the law of cause and effect.

When you are giving more to others, you are indirectly saying to the Universe, "I am wealthy and I can afford to give to others."

Since every thought is a prayer, the Universe will return more wealth to you. It is only when you give away your prosperity that you make room for more prosperity to come into your life. This is the apparent paradox of creating greater prosperity. To get more, you need to give more.

As noted earlier, your prosperity-limiting beliefs will also be tested by painful, angry experiences so that you may become aware of them. Let us tell you a story of Linda (not her real name) who was able to productively channel her anger regarding her husband's mismanagement of household finances. We think this is an important example because one of the top reasons for divorce in the United States (about 50 percent of all marriages) is due to financial issues.

A lot of anger and negative energy is generated when household partners argue about finances. On the surface it may be about spending too much or spending too little. However, it is really about underlying limiting beliefs about prosperity and self-esteem. At the end of the day it may have nothing to do with money.

Linda was a nurse in a hospital and Jack was a physician. Linda had her own savings plan in the hospital where she was diligently putting away a certain percentage of her income. Although she managed her own savings plan, she left all other financial dealings in the household to her husband.

Her faith in her husband's management of household finances was, however, shaken when he started to invest in highly risky stocks. The problem began in the last quarter of 1999 when the prices of technology stocks began to rise very rapidly. In order to take advantage of the rising stock prices, Jack put more of their joint income and savings into such stocks.

As the months progressed, Jack was spending more and more time trading in dubious technology stocks and using their joint income for such purposes. Linda felt increasingly uncomfortable in such a situation and expressed her concern that Jack should stop getting so attached to the stock market. She argued that they should invest their savings instead in more "conservative and diversified" investments; however, her advice fell on deaf ears as Jack continued to trade in highly risky stocks.

While Jack was interested in saving for investment purposes, he was critical of Linda's spending habits since the beginning of their marriage. Whenever Linda wanted to buy something for herself, he would question her purchases, always asking whether they really "needed" it. Many household items that Linda considered necessary from an aesthetic point of view was considered "wasteful" and "nonpractical" from Jack's viewpoint. Linda also wanted to finish their basement, but Jack did not think it was necessary. Linda grew increasingly tired of listening to Jack's criticism. She began to wonder why she needed to get permission to spend income that she earned herself.

When technology stocks took a downturn in the autumn of 2000, Linda became infuriated that Jack had lost a large percentage of the value of their joint savings and had failed to listen to her earlier advice. Linda, however, turned her fury into an opportunity to become more financially independent.

It was during this time that Linda came to us for advice. We recommended that she become more financially literate and take a more active interest in managing the household finances. In order for her to become more financially literate, we recommended two books to her. One book was *Smart Women Become Rich* by David Bach. The other book was by Suze Orman called *The Courage to Be Rich*. We also recommended that Linda research the Internet to find out about diversified mutual funds that had performed well over the last 10 years.

Although Linda was already aware that investing regular amounts (known as *dollar cost averaging*) in a diversified mutual fund would, over a period of many years, literally lead to millions of dollars due to the power of interest compounding, reading these books reinforced and confirmed what she already knew. She also searched the Internet and found mutual funds that had performed well over the last decade.

Once Linda was armed with financial knowledge, she felt confident to notify Jack that she was going to stop putting her own income into individual stocks. She also persuaded him to put his own savings into the mutual funds that she had done research on. Jack agreed to Linda's plan of action. Jack clearly acknowledged his own greed and his attachment to money.

His desire to control his stocks and his inability to do so was a deeply humbling experience. He agreed with Linda that a "let go and let God" approach to investing was a more peaceful strategy. By investing a set amount each month in a mutual fund, no matter what the stock market did, he was free of the tension that was part of monitoring the price movements of individual stocks.

An additional benefit of this financial disaster was that Jack became less critical of Linda's own spending. Linda also reinforced this by making it clear to Jack that she was not going to take Jack's criticism and resistance to her purchases anymore. To demonstrate this, she made some "aesthetic" purchases to which Jack had previously resisted. She felt empowered as she made these spending decisions on her own. Why did she need Jack's approval to spend her own income? Further, they were already putting away a reasonable percentage for retirement.

Another piece of advice we gave Linda was to use her feelings as a guide to make the right spending decisions. If what we are about to buy gives us unpleasant feelings such as anxiety or turmoil, then it is not the right spending decision. Typically, the ego aspect of us wants us to buy "status" symbol goods that separate us from other human beings by making us feel superior.

Whenever we want to feel superior over others by buying things, our feelings will usually be unpleasant, even if it comes in the mildest form. On the other hand, if luxury items truly nourish our minds and souls, and they are something we can afford, then we are making the right spending decision. What may be a luxury for one person may be a necessity for another.

In the end, instead of blaming Jack, Linda was able to productively channel her anger by taking more financial responsibility. By doing so, she felt financially empowered. More importantly, Linda's action also had a positive impact on Jack, who began to understand the true nature of abundance. This financial disaster and Linda's associated anger was a gift. It was a gift because it led them toward the path of prosperity.

Let us summarize, therefore, some of the key benefits that Linda and Jack were able to get by Linda's initiative to productively channel her anger. Although they lost a lot of money in the stock market, they were able to gain other elements of prosperity consciousness, such as the following:

- Greater self-esteem for Linda because of her courage to take action.
- An understanding that earning true wealth requires patience.
- A more loving and respectful spousal relationship.
- Better physical health for Linda. If Linda had suppressed her anger, this could have eventually led to diseases such as depression and heart disease.
- Greater peace of mind for both of them, enabling them to sleep better. Good sleep equals good health and great wealth.

Anger may make us more aware that we need to be financially responsible for ourselves. It may also teach us that there are other elements of prosperity over and above money.

11

ANGER AS A PATHWAY TO BALANCE IN LIFE

$\mathscr{F}$requent irritation and impatience are forms of anger, although on a milder scale. As noted in Chapter 2, harboring such feelings on a continuous basis is a precursor of a host of diseases, including heart disease, depression, and insomnia. These feelings could be symptoms of stress, often due to an unbalanced lifestyle. According to the American Psychological Association, it has been estimated that more than 75 percent of all physician office visits are for stress-related complaints.

Balance refers to the total harmony of your soul, mind, and body. If you face anger and frequent irritation, it may be a message that you need to examine whether you have balance in your life. It may be possible that you are concentrating most of your life energies in one area to the neglect of other areas. A common reason why life is not in balance for many people is that too much of their time is spent working to meet ego needs such as the next bigger car, the newest gadget, or the latest fashion.

Let us stress here that there is nothing wrong per se in having and pursuing material things. Material things are condensed energy and are a part of Infinite Intelligence, as you will recall from Chapter 4. The issue is whether you are using most of your energies to pursue these needs at the expense of your soul. Your wholeness comes from balancing the needs of your soul, mind, and body. In other words, **it is okay from a spiritual standpoint to** *enjoy all the material abundance you want;* **however, you should not sell your spirit to get that material abundance.** This is the meaning of the biblical scriptural saying, "Be in this world, but not of this world."

If you think that recurrent anger or irritation may be due to the fact that your life is not in harmony, go back to Chapter 9, "Anger as a Pathway to Freedom from Inner Addictions" and reflect on the inner addictions you may need to release. Your outward imbalance is once again a reflection of inner imbalance of too many false beliefs. If you are addicted to your job, money, or societal status, ask yourself the following questions:

- Do I really need to put in those extra hours on my job? Is the extra income compromising my quality of life and a harmonious lifestyle?
- Do I really need that promotion? If I were to get promoted, what would it mean in terms of extra responsibility and the impact of that on my stress level? Do I want a promotion so that I can "get ahead" and look good in front of others, or is it because I feel that I should be genuinely rewarded for good work?
- In order to bring balance in my life, can I take advantage of opportunities that my company may offer me such as working at home or job sharing? Many companies have these opportunities in place. Don't be afraid to ask your boss. You won't get anything in life unless you ask for it.

We are both professionals who are also parents of two small children. We, therefore, understand the plight of many working couples and how difficult it is to juggle careers, family, and self-nurture in a balancing act. One of the most frequent complaints we hear from people is that they don't have enough time to give sufficient attention to their families or to nurture themselves. This is indirectly saying that work is more important than their family. Let us give you some tips that we practice. These suggestions may help you reduce some of your stress and related irritation and anger.

TIPS TO FINDING TIME TO CARE FOR YOUR LOVED ONES

An action that has freed up a lot of time in our lives is the fact that we have cut down on watching TV, especially in the evenings. We are not condemning watching TV or asking you to give up all your sit-coms. What is important is that you should be aware of *what* you watch and *how much* you watch. The average American household has the TV on for 7 hours per day. An extra hour saved on not watching TV can be spent in productive family time. Here is what you can do with an extra hour of saved time:

- **Discuss family activities** that occurred during the day (15 minutes). Do this after dinner. Make sure the TV is turned off while you talk to each other. Background TV noise can prevent focused listening. Its noise can be toxic to your brain, too.
- **Talk with your spouse or partner** about daily activities (15 minutes). Lack of heart-to-heart communication among spouses can be a reason for potential anger and resentment. It is important to sit down and talk to each other, even if there are no "issues." If you are fortunate to have a happy marriage, don't take it for granted. Marriage or any significant long-term relationship is like a plant. If you don't water and nourish it on a regular basis, it will die. Anger can be a symptom that you are not nourishing your relationship. Heart-to-heart communication is one key nutrient to the plant of your relationship.
- **Read to your child daily** (15 minutes). When one parent is reading, for example, to the younger one, the other parent might help the older child practice the piano.

- **Help your child with homework** (15 minutes). Even if they can do it by themselves, make sure you check it before it is put in their schoolbag. It has been shown in many studies that children of parents who take an active interest in their education do well in their studies and life in general.

As you can see, you can achieve a lot in an hour. Modify this example to your needs. Here are other tips you can use during the day to build closer ties to your family members and relieve the frustration and anger of not being able to spend enough time with your loved ones.

- **Take your children on errands.** While in the car, make it a point to really listen to them. Make sure there are no distractions such as the radio. If they are old enough, you can also use this time to give them spelling and math quizzes, or simply let them tell you a story.
- **Spend time together in the garden.** Even if your garden consists of a few potted plants in the balcony, the entire family can get together to "stop and smell the roses." If you have a backyard, you can work together. Make your children observant of nature in action, such as watching an earthworm or ladybug, or examining the individual seeds of a dried dandelion.
- **Develop a similar hobby with your child or spouse.** Recently I (Reshmi) took up learning the piano with my daughter purely for the sake of enjoyment and learning something new. It motivates both of us to learn and encourages bonding between us.
- **Don't forget your extended family.** Your nephews and nieces, in-laws, aunts and uncles, and grandparents are part of your extended family. Make it a point to meet with them on a regular basis. Hosting a potluck gathering can reduce the stress of trying to do everything yourself.

- **Send love cards and notes on a regular basis.** Do this for your children, your spouse, and extended family on a regular basis. Don't just wait for special occasions such as birthdays. Send a "Thinking of You" card or send an e-mail or electronic card. Reward your child for doing something good and give them a card to reinforce the good behavior.

TIPS TO TAKE CARE OF YOURSELF

Even if you have time to care for your loved ones, your life will not be in balance if you don't have the time to care for yourself. We have seen this happen in many women. These women often feel resentful because they look after the needs of everyone else except themselves. In such cases, these women are fused with their roles as mothers and spouses.

If you are one of these women, angry feelings may be an indication that you need to find more time for yourself and detach yourself from your usual role. If you identify solely with your role as a caregiver, you have in effect an inner addiction. Your anger is telling you to release these addictions. Here are some common limiting beliefs:

- My child's need always comes first.
- I have to be the perfect mother/spouse.
- I should not be enjoying myself at the expense of my child.
- I am not a good mother.
- I have to give my child my full attention because I did not get enough attention when I was a child.
- I have to give my children enough extracurricular activities to keep up with my neighbors.

There are many variations on the same theme. If you think you have any of these beliefs, turn them around into something positive such as "**I am a good mother,**" or "**I love myself and need to**

take care of myself." Repeat them on a daily basis. See Chapter 8 on "Anger as a Pathway to Self-Esteem." Take the positive affirmations from that section and repeat them as well. The following are practical tips on caring for yourself that you can do in addition to your affirmations. Actions are quite powerful and will help you to achieve your goal of inner peace rather than affirmations alone.

- **Take a power nap during the day.** If you feel you are not getting enough sleep during the night because you are stressed out, you may want to take a short nap of not more than half an hour between the hours of 1 P.M. to 3 P.M. Many sleep medicine studies have shown that people feel more rejuvenated and alert after such naps. Your threshold for anger and irritation will also be higher during the evening hours when you interact with loved ones.[1]
- **Do short meditations before leaving work.** When you are tired after a long day of work, it is more likely that you will have a lower threshold to become reactive to loved ones when you go home. A 5-minute meditation has a calming influence. It has certainly proved to be effective for us. If you don't have a private office, you can meditate in your car in the parking lot or in your garage.
- **Watch a funny movie.** Laughter releases chemicals in your body known as endorphins. These make you feel relaxed. Your threshold for irritation and anger will be lower.
- **Read a book or listen to a tape on spirituality and self-help.** Reading these kinds of books will make you more conscious about the importance of taking care of yourself and enable you to see yourself as divine. Even if you spend only half an hour each day reading these kinds of books, you will

[1]Please visit our Web site, www.SleepHealthDoc.com, to get your free special report on how to get quality sleep for good health.

end up with more than a month of reading in a year, the equivalent of four 40-hour work weeks!!

- **Take a hot bath with scented candles lighted around your tub.** Also use scented soaps. Both scented soaps and candles will give you pleasant sensations, it is essentially a form of aromatherapy. You may also use scented candles while you are reading your self-help books.

- **Get a new look.** You don't have to spend a fortune to do this. You can get a new haircut or new shoes, as well as a bottle of cologne or perfume. If you are a woman, treat yourself to a new scarf and new shades of lipstick and blush. You will be amazed how so little can make you feel so good about yourself.

- **Do regular mindfulness meditation.** Walk in nature and listen to peaceful music. Do these activities with whole-hearted attention. As we will discuss in Part III, these are all forms of meditation. Meditation is not confined to repeating words and sitting in a Buddha-like position.

- **Do not answer phone calls an hour after coming home from work.** Your energy level is likely to be low during this time. You don't have to exert yourself by answering the phone. Let the caller leave a message and return the call when you are more relaxed.

- **Limit the extracurricular activities of your children so you have more time to yourself.** We see too many women these days packing their children's nonschool time with extracurricular activities. A lot of time is spent on chauffeuring them to various places. We are not condemning extracurricular activities, we are just asking that you limit them so that you can find time for yourself and let your children **be** rather than always **do.** Children need ample opportunity to play by themselves, which can be a highly creative activity.

All the actions just listed can go a long way toward boosting your self-esteem and restoring a sense that you deserve to be pampered. We have seen many women who spend their lives giving all their energies to their spouses or children. In other words, they are addicted to their roles as caregivers. When the children leave the nest, they feel an enormous sense of loss, frustration, and anger. They feel anger because they denied themselves and could not realize their own dreams. This, in turn, often leads to depression.

There also could be imbalance in someone's life if they are too "spiritual." There are people (although they are a minority) who have given up all material pursuits because they consider it "bad." However, this kind of belief is likely to lead to an unbalanced lifestyle. As you will recall, balance is harmony of your soul, mind, and **body.** Pursuing material and bodily needs is also important for overall harmony. However, it is important to keep the pursuit of material needs in perspective.

You can find the right balance in your life to love yourself, be a loving caregiver, a productive worker, and a valued community member at the same time. It is possible to have it all. Your goal in life is that all of these should be expanding in a balanced way. This is where creativity comes in. The next chapter will show how you can use your anger as an important step towards an ever-increasing creative life.

Anger may be an indication that our priorities are not in balance in our life. If recognized and acknowledged, anger can help us restore our spiritual, emotional, and physical harmony.

12

ANGER AS A PATHWAY TO CREATIVITY

*I*f you think that creativity is an idea that is confined to music and the arts in general, think again. To us, creativity means making room for something new and better in one's life. Most of us, however, like to hang on to what we have been doing. In other words, we don't like to change for the better; i.e., we hold on to security. Creativity is, therefore, the opposite of security. If you are not changing and growing to improve every area of your life, you are going against the natural flow of the Universe. Everything in the Universe is in a constant flux of change and growth, down to the tiniest atoms and electrons.

One of the first things that you have to realize is that your mind has an infinite capacity to create. Many studies, however, have shown that the average person uses only 5 percent of their total mental capacity. Surprising, is it not? What happens if you don't use your brains for creative activity? Brain research has shown that people who do not use their brains creatively are at greater risk of Alzheimer's disease than those who are mentally active in a creative way.

Alzheimer's disease is a degenerative disease whereby a person suffers from gradual loss of brain functions. It is a debilitating disease that already afflicts millions of elderly Americans each year and is an enormous burden to the caregivers of these persons. In simple terms, if you don't use your brain, you will lose it.

A common reason why most people do not use their creative capabilities is because they *believe* they are not creative. Once again any anger you feel by not fulfilling your dreams is simply a message that you need to release the limiting beliefs you have in your subconscious mind. Here are some mistaken beliefs on creativity:

- I don't have the talent to be a writer/musician/artist.
- Most artists are poor, therefore I should not pursue this path.
- I will never succeed in a creative endeavor.
- My spouse/friends will laugh at me if I try this new activity.
- I don't have the time to pursue creative activities.

As you can see, these are common limiting beliefs on creativity based on certain professions. We would like you to broaden your view of creativity and think about how you can be more creative in all areas of your life. Let us stress that you should never compare yourself with other people regarding how you are doing. That is what the ego likes to do. It is not a competitive race, although the ego likes to think it is.

Each individual has unique God-given talents. Your job is to give birth to those talents and develop them to their fullest, infinite potential. If you want to be a creative person, you should **compare yourself to what you** *used to be.* Given this framework, you can use the following statements as affirmations to ingrain into your subconscious:

- **I am a better/creative gardener.**
- **I am a better/creative parent.**
- **I am a better/creative worker.**
- **I am a better/creative spouse/lover.**
- **I am a better/creative communicator.**
- **I am a better/creative friend.**
- **I am a better/creative businessperson.**

• **I am a better/creative writer/musician/artist.**
• **I am a better/creative cook.**

And the list can go on. The most important point is that you should take baby steps to realize your creativity. **It is the small steps, day in and day out, that you take that makes the big difference in final results.** This is what we do when we learn to play a new piece of music on the piano. We learn note-by-note, measure-by-measure. We also teach our daughter this way.

This is how most of the great masters in any field achieve what they have achieved. They do it step-by-step and in a consistent way. Don't try to do everything at once, or otherwise it will become overwhelming. When we try to do too many things at once and want to be good at everything, we lose balance. Your anger and irritation will tell you when you are off course. You just need to listen to your feelings.

Since most of us are stuck in our old ways, one way the Universe prods us to change and be creative is through our anger. Let me relate an incident to you about how I used my own anger to enhance my life and be more creative. After getting my master's degree from Oxford University, I did not feel it was necessary to pursue a doctorate. My father, who had a doctorate, encouraged me to pursue one when I got married. However, I still could not be convinced and remained quite comfortable with my education. Shortly after my marriage, I got a job and worked under a supervisor who happened to have a doctorate.

After working there for a short while, I had a rude awakening. The people who were getting promoted in the organization had more advanced degrees than myself, such as a doctorate. Further, some of them appeared to be less competent than myself. It angered me to realize that it was not enough to be intrinsically smart and intelligent. The world, with all its superficialities, placed a lot of value on degrees and titles.

While I was working in this company, Mahmood, who was just finishing up his training in internal medicine, got a fellowship to do further medical training at Case Western Reserve University in Cleveland, Ohio. I, therefore, did not have any other choice but to follow him. Should I apply for a job in Cleveland, or should I get a doctorate degree at the university? The choice was clear. I was going to get a doctorate, even if it meant 3 years of hard work.

A doctorate involves original research and the creative application of knowledge to a particular research problem or issue. In other words, I used my anger as a path towards expanding my creative intelligence. While the original motivation for getting the degree was not to be mistreated in the future, doing the thesis work was fulfilling, as I was able to make an original contribution. The doctorate also laid the foundation for me to do more advanced scientific work, another fulfilling avenue of creativity.

This personal experience provides a positive example of how we can use anger to further our creativity. As mentioned before, however, creativity is not limited to pursuing an advanced degree or further education. It can touch all areas of our lives. Anger can give us the fuel to run our creative ship. If we do not want to use that fuel, we then choose to stay in a safe harbor. After a while this can feel stifling. If, however, we power our ship with the fuel of anger, we can move on to open seas. The possibilities of what we can then achieve with our lives are limitless.

Let us recall that Infinite Intelligence, by definition, is an open sea of creative energy. Each human being is a drop in that sea. By being creative, we are in the open sea of our souls, and this is the most natural state of our being. Staying in safe harbor means that we are creating an artificial boundary for our souls, which by definition is without boundary. By being creative, we can break conventional boundaries, which can benefit ourselves as well as others.

An example of how creativity through anger can benefit others is this book. Throughout our careers we never dreamed of engaging in popular writing. Our safe harbor was our scientific writing. However, only recently our souls beckoned us to go into this new venture by asking us the question, "Why not?". (The soul, by the way, will never ask the question "Why?".) In fact, by openly discussing our personal anger struggles in a public forum such as this book, we hope we will be able to heal others.

Writing this book has not been easy. Having full-time jobs and managing two small children meant that only late evenings and weekends were made available for writing it. It also meant that we had to use vacation time to write. It required focus and determination to silence the voices of our demons, which said, "You can't write this, as you are not an expert or guru," or "You are too tired."

When you know that your heart burns with a flame that does not flicker, you know that you are doing the work of your soul. This is when, no matter how hard the winds of doubt, lethargy, criticism, or excuses blow, the flame within your heart continues to burn unabated. This is called *passion.*

Most of us too often give in to our demons of excuses. During such times, we have to be more vigilant and take action to counter such thoughts. I, for example, during the early phases of this book, on many occasions took up my pen and forced myself to write to fight thoughts of lethargy. Once, however, the chapters started coming together, it was an extremely enjoyable process that involved being in a state of "flow." In other words, writing no longer seemed to be hard work, as it appeared to be coming out from my heart.

I would also like to add that some of the chapters of this book "unfolded" as I was in the process of writing. When I was stung by a wasp because of how I mismanaged my anger as described in Chapter 13, I thought, "Good, I have some more material for this book." The pain from this experience was turned into an opportunity.

When we transform our anger into a creative experience that can help others, it becomes one of the highest forms of love. One aspect of creativity is that we become open to love in all its forms. In the next chapter we will discuss how you can be an open and creative person when it comes to compassion, and how your anger may help you develop this quality.

Anger can be used as the fuel for transporting our souls to the boundless sea of creativity. By being creative, we not only serve ourselves, we serve humanity.

13

ANGER AS A PATHWAY TO COMPASSION AND UNDERSTANDING

*S*ometimes the purpose of our anger is to teach us understanding and compassion. Unless we walk in someone
else's shoes, it is very difficult to appreciate their problem, or their
point of view. Too often, we see other people through the narrow
lens of our own eyes. Because our vision is sometimes narrow, we
may have a tendency to impose judgment without trying to see the
issue from the other person's frame of reference.

If anger arises when we are judgmental, it may be an indication that we need to be more understanding. In the first place, it
may signify that we need to communicate with the "perpetrator"
to get more information regarding why that person is behaving the
way they are. Secondly, it might be an indication for us to step back
and look at ourselves to see how we are responsible for generating
such a situation.

The issue of understanding is important in the workplace
where we spend much of our time. Having the capacity to see the
point of view of our peers, bosses, and those who work under us is
critical for generating harmonious relationships as well as ensur-
ing peace of mind.

More important though, it could have a significant effect on
your career. In his best-selling book, *Working with Emotional
Intelligence,* Daniel Goleman researched many companies in the
United States and came to the conclusion that one of the charac-

teristics of true top performers was empathy. Empathy means the ability to be aware of how someone else feels and what their needs and concerns are. Goleman also found that the top performers were able to manage their emotions such as anger and ensure win-win results when there was conflict.

In order to help you understand how you can use your anger to lead to a better understanding in the workplace, let us narrate a story of how one worker angered and "betrayed" the other. It will also illustrate the importance of how you may need to take personal responsibility in work-related conflicts.

John and Ben were two coworkers who had worked together on a successful project that had won much acclaim in their company. During John's annual performance review, however, John was surprised to find that he had received negative feedback from a coworker; because of this, his boss gave him an "unsatisfactory" rating as he was not meeting "the needs of a customer."

The annual performance appraisal took into account the feedback of peers and colleagues from different departments, including the person's own department. Although the feedback was supposed to be confidential, his boss gave him enough clues to let him know it was Ben.

John was shocked and angered that he had been "betrayed." He was also angry with his boss because his boss placed so much importance on one feedback and failed to take into account his overall contribution. John had given positive feedback on Ben, but Ben was stabbing him in the back.

For many months, John held a strong grudge against Ben and felt victimized by the situation. On one occasion, however, John had an opportunity to talk to another coworker who knew Ben quite well. He learned from this conversation that Ben had a difficult childhood, which led him to be overly critical about people. It was the first time that John had a clearer vision of Ben, and was able to have compassion for him. He was finally able to let go of his resentment toward Ben.

It was around this time that John came to discuss this situation with us. We asked him whether in the past *he* had betrayed or victimized anyone. He confessed that he had, although it was done in a personal relationship rather than in a work setting. We explained to him that this was the law of cause and effect that was working in his life.

John acknowledged that he now knew how it felt to be betrayed and vowed that he would make every attempt not to repeat such behavior in the future. In the end, this resentful situation led to an understanding not only of his coworker, but also of himself. He learned the importance of personal responsibility through this experience.

As we explained before, people in relationships are mirrors of each other. What we do not like in someone else is something that we do not like in ourselves. It is usually some aspect of ourselves that we are not aware of that wants recognition and healing. By seeing the pattern or quality reflected in someone else, we are given an opportunity to recognize that same quality within ourselves. From a spiritual perspective, John "needed" Ben to come into his life at the time he did to teach him compassion and the need to understand that he should stop victimizing other people.

One of the most common ways we arouse anger in ourselves is when we try to prove others wrong, or prove ourselves right, especially through an argument. This happens because we are not willing to accept another person's opinions and beliefs. The fact that we think someone is "wrong" is essentially a form of judgment. Even if they are "wrong," it is important to step back and ask whether it is worth creating a tense situation.

Too often our egos, or the "I" aspect of us, wants to feel superior by winning an argument; however, this kind of thinking only causes separation. As we noted earlier, we are not separate from one another. Furthermore, even if we have won an argument, we really haven't won in a true sense, because we may make the other person feel small, as well as possibly causing resentment and bitterness.

An occasion when I had to prove "my" way occurred when my daughter, Rania, was about 4 years old. This event angered me and taught me a lot about myself regarding how I could have been less judgmental and more compassionate.

It was a summer evening when I made some chocolate milk for Rania after she requested it. After I made the milk and she tasted it, she did not want it. Despite adjusting the sugar in the milk three times, Rania did not drink it. The first time I added half a teaspoon it was, "It does not taste good." The second time it was, "It's too cold." The third time it was, "It still does not taste good."

Each time she refused to drink the milk, my irritation level rose. By the third time, I was quite exasperated and I told her in a raised voice to go to bed, despite the fact it was about 2 hours before her regular bedtime. After another heated exchange between mother and daughter, Rania went upstairs to her room.

Obviously feeling angry, I went outside in the sunroom to get some fresh air and to think about this situation. The last couple of months I had been trying hard to be more creative and responsible in my reactions to my children; however, this time around, I realized that I had not given the best possible response. I realized that I was fixated on making sure that my children received their supply of calcium and protein.

For the first time, I questioned why I was so fixated about my beliefs on my children's nutrition. I realized that not having milk for a day would not have a negative effect on my daughter's health. I also realized that it was important to accept my daughter for who she was—just a little girl. If she did not want the milk, why force the issue and cause so much tension?

Still feeling unsettled, I went out to weed the garden after sitting on the porch for a while. Near the exterior of the sunroom was a wasp nest. It had been there for the last 4 years and the wasps had never bothered the family. As I bent down to pull out some weeds on a flowerbed beside the nest, I felt a very sharp sting on my upper back. Suddenly, I realized that a wasp had stung me. I raced upstairs to Mahmood to show him my back. Seeing a red inflamed patch on my upper back, he treated me with some medicine and put an ice pack on it to prevent further inflammation.

It was the first time in my life I had been stung by a wasp. I immediately saw the connection between the "sting" that I gave my daughter, and the sting that I received from the wasp. The inflammation that occurred on my skin was symbolic of the anger I did not express responsibly to my daughter. I had certainly learned my lesson.

If you think a conversation you are about to have is going to lead to tense feelings, the simple course of action is to accept the other person for what he or she says and to let go of your need to be right. In the words of Dr. Wayne Dyer, it is "better to be kind rather than to be right." You can improve your relationships if you try this.

Our marital relationship has improved to a significant degree by practicing such a principle. Many potential fights have been avoided by letting go of the need to be right. In situations where an angry exchange is about to happen, one of us has physically walked away, changed the subject, or has explicitly acknowledged that the conversation is heading in the wrong direction.

The most important aspect of avoiding such confrontations is the ability to recognize and be aware that the conversation is heading toward the wrong direction. Recognizing the direction of your feelings does this. As we mentioned before, human feelings are like a barometer to help us make the right choices. There are basically two types of feelings: pleasant and unpleasant.

A pleasant feeling means that you are making the right choices in terms of what you are thinking, saying, or doing. A "right" choice is a choice that will generate harmony for you and others. An unpleasant feeling, like anger, means that you may not be making the right choices. If during a conversation you are feeling angry, step back and reevaluate what you are saying. Even if you have not said anything, but the thinking itself is generating the unpleasant feelings, then what you are thinking may not be on the right lines. This indicates that you need to choose thoughts that will bring you peace.

We would like to end this chapter by noting that true understanding of another person occurs when we realize that person is Spirit in material disguise. The opposite of understanding is judgment. Judgment implies that we label people with words such as "bad", "horrible", or "obnoxious."

Whenever we label someone in a judgmental way, it means that we create boundaries between that person and ourselves. From a spiritual standpoint, there are no boundaries because life is one universal flow. The spiritual challenge is to suspend judgment and to see beyond the physical illusion of separation. Our anger can help us toward this goal if we choose to.

Anger can teach us how to understand the viewpoint of others. It may indicate that we need to be less judgmental and more accepting of others and ourselves. By being able to understand our own divinity, we will have the capacity to understand the divinity in others.

14

ANGER AS A PATHWAY TO PRESENT MOMENT AWARENESS

*L*ife is a series of moments—it is one moment after another. One spiritual challenge of life is to live and enjoy each moment to the fullest extent. Most of us, however, are thinking of things that happened yesterday or are worrying about events that have not happened. When we do this, our minds are distracted and we can't enjoy what is happening right now. If you think about it, Infinite Intelligence is in everyone, everything, and everywhere. It is also timeless. You, too, are part of this infinity and eternity.

From this perspective of infinity, one moment is really no better or worse than another moment because every moment or bit of time is contained in you and Infinite Intelligence at the same time. Every moment is sacred and every experience is sacred. The problem arises because of how you choose to label and think about each moment and your mistaken belief that you are separate from your source of Infinite Intelligence.

Did you know that almost 20 million Americans have chronic insomnia (the inability to fall asleep or stay asleep)? Another 60 million Americans suffer from intermittent and transient insomnia. A common reason why people can't go to sleep is because of anxiety.[1] Anxiety is chronic fear and worry that something bad is

---

[1]Please visit our Web site, www.SleepHealthDoc.com, to get your free special report on how to get quality sleep for good health.

going to happen. Because of insufficient sleep, the threshold for irritability and anger is higher during the day. In such cases your anger may be telling you that you need to release thoughts of worry and get back into the present. If you don't release thoughts of anxiety, it could have negative effects on your health, such as:

- Risk of heart disease. A number of public health studies have confirmed that anxiety alone can have a significant negative effect on your heart.
- A weakened immune system and risk of infections due to lack of sleep caused by anxiety.
- Risk of depression and mental illness.

Aside from these health effects, your outer experience in life in terms of your relationships or career will also be affected negatively by anxiety. Remember, thoughts are things. The more you think about something, the more likely it is going to happen because you are a cocreator of your life. In other words, what you think about becomes self-fulfilling, especially if you think about it too much.

For all these reasons, it is important that you listen to your anger when you are anxious and heed its message to help you come back to present moment awareness. Have you had an experience when you were thinking about something negative and it happened? Your response could have been, " I knew this was going to happen." Now you know the reason why things like this happen. So be careful of what you think about.

One way to train your mind to focus on the present moment is **mindful meditation.** In the broadest sense, mindful meditation is the practice of putting your whole-hearted attention on whatever you are doing or not doing now. As we will show you in Part III, you can practice this kind of meditation while you are eating, drinking, playing with your children, or taking a nature walk. Not only does meditation have a positive effect in helping you to become less reactive when you are angry, it will also help your mind focus on the present so that it does not wander off with worrisome thoughts.

One practical step that will train you to focus on the present moment is **mindful listening.** Often when we are listening to another person, we are preparing our response to them or our mind is busy with other thoughts. This is not really listening because we are not paying wholehearted attention to what they are saying. In addition to helping you achieve present moment awareness, mindful listening also signifies that you really care about the person and you wish to understand them in depth. As your understanding grows, your relationship will also flourish.

A key step in mindful listening is that you should repeat or restate what the other person is saying. You do this until they nod or say yes. Here are some examples of statements that reflect back what the other person has said:

- I hear that you are saying . . .
- If I am correct, you mean that . . .
- I understand that your concern or issue is . . .
- I understand that you feel . . .

These are a few examples of statements that you can use to practice mindful listening, which in turn will help you get back to present moment awareness. In Chapter 19 we will discuss how you can use some of these techniques to practice compassionate communication when you have a disagreement or conflict that generates anger.

The other type of mental activity that takes us away from the present moment is when we hold on to the "psychic baggage" of resentment or guilt, usually due to past hurt. Resentment is anger that has never been expressed. Because the burden of the "baggage" may be so great, we cannot enjoy ourselves and live *now*. We relive those moments in our minds as if they were real.

As Dr. Wayne Dyer has so aptly described in his book, *Your Sacred Self,* our past can be thought of as the wake of a boat. The wake is the trail that is left behind by a moving boat. Our memories of past events can be similarly thought of as trails that have been left behind. Just as the trail of the boat does not have any influence on which way the boat is going to move now, our memories should not have an influence on how we should live now.

If we want to live in the present moment it is important that we release all resentment through forgiveness. The anger we experience when we have been unjustly treated or hurt may indicate that we have to learn how to forgive. Forgiveness means that we release blame. It means letting go. When we have been seemingly hurt by others and we feel angry about it, **this anger may indicate that (a) we need to learn the lesson from the experience; (b) take appropriate action (or inaction) based on compassion and understanding; and (c) let go.**

This is basically a three-step process for forgiveness and releasing blame. If all three steps are followed, then angry situations in the future are unlikely to show up; however, if one has taken the first step without taking the next two steps, the spiritual test is not over. Events that generate anger will continue to happen until a person develops the qualities of forgiveness and mercy.

Forgiveness does not mean that we condone or accept wrongdoing. It does not mean that we should not lock up a "criminal" if we have to. It means that we see the innocence of the soul behind the personality or ego. On a spiritual plane, our worst "enemy" and the saint are one and the same. How can this be? If you refer back to Figure 2 in Chapter 4, you will see the Universe, including us, comprises one sea of conscious energy. In other words, from an energy standpoint, there is no difference between a "criminal" and a "saint."

This is the reason why taking revenge and hurting someone back when they have hurt you never works in the long run. Ultimately, you will end up hurting yourself more. In other words, the law of cause and effect comes into play. A wiser approach is to take action that is based on understanding and get to the "root causes" regarding why someone is behaving the way they do. It means that you should imagine yourself in the other person's shoes as well as communicate with that person. How to communicate compassionately is discussed in Part III.

In the case of our ex-accountant who charged us an unjustifiable bill for his services, the three-step process of forgiveness involved: (a) learning not to be victims; (b) taking action by **not** writing an angry letter, but a polite yet firm one; and (c) letting go and forgiving.

Even though an event may have happened long ago, and the "culprit" is no longer in our lives, we may still hold on to resentment. Although the incident may have been forgotten or does not have any significance for us anymore, it is a good idea to go back in our memory bank and forgive that person. Unless you do so, the blocked energy of resentment will remain within you. Either of two things will happen: it might materialize as disease, or angry events will occur in the future in order for you to learn the lesson of forgiveness.

If you are able to cultivate the qualities of mercy, compassion, creativity, and prosperity consciousness as well as a belief that you are infinite in nature, you will be able to understand the meaning of unconditional love, which is the topic of the next chapter.

Anger can help us realize that we are not living with our full attention in the present moment. Life is a series of moments. The spiritual challenge is to live in each moment without being distracted by the future or our past. Anger can help us to cultivate qualities of forgiveness and mercy.

15

ANGER AS A PATHWAY TO UNCONDITIONAL LOVE

*B*efore this chapter on unconditional love was written, an incident occurred involving our then 2½-year-old son, Ryan. It was about noon when I was finishing my lunch in the kitchen. Ryan, who was initially playing downstairs in the kitchen area, disappeared from sight. I called out to him, but there was no response. Since I assumed he went upstairs, I quickly went upstairs, as I did not want to leave him unsupervised.

The master bedroom door was open; I could see Ryan playing on the carpet floor with things he had taken out from my handbag. Aside from the dollar bills, my cellular phone, and coins, Ryan had also taken out my red lipstick and had drawn big marks with it on the carpet.

I quickly went to the bathroom and got some wet towels and started to wipe the marks off. As I did so, I picked up Ryan and gave him a kiss. I also popped a mint in his mouth, which was still in my bag. With the mint in his mouth, Ryan grinned with a big smile, totally unaware of the mishap he had created. During this time, I did not feel any anger at all, and was very aware of myself.

What was truly amazing was the parallel in this incident with another one that happened almost 2 years ago involving Rania, my daughter, who was then almost 3 years old. While I had gone to wash my hands in the bathroom, Rania helped herself to my oil paintbrushes, which were left exposed on my palette. Further,

Rania painted *red* marks on virtually the same carpet spot as Ryan had done with the lipstick. During that time, however, I was reactive and gave Rania a lecture as well as time out. Fortunately, the paint marks were removable with turpentine.

This time around, I could clearly see the message from the Universe. The thought that came across to me during this incident was, "Look how you've improved. Look at the big change in yourself." The same situation was being repeated so that I could be given an opportunity to see my new inner-self being reflected back to me.

The state of being when we pour out love no matter what happens is the state of *unconditional love*. This is what it means when our purpose in life is to become vessels of love, as we mentioned in the introduction of this book. "Unconditional" means to be without conditions. It means no strings attached or no boundaries. This is when anger has transformed itself into true love, which has no boundaries. It is the state when we feel there is no difference between "me" and "you." We feel the "me" and "you" are exactly one and the same. It is a natural state when we want to serve others. When we serve others, we serve ourselves.

Another way of looking at unconditional love is to refer to Figure 2 in Chapter 4. When you are **aware** each moment that you are part of Infinite Intelligence, that is also a state of unconditional love. This state of love occurs when you don't forget for a second that you are divine and that you view every experience in life as sacred.

Your ego, or the small "i," is not vanquished but is merged with the big "I" of Infinite Intelligence. In one sense your ego is given ultimately what it wants—total dominance. However, it is a dominance that is not based on fear and separation, but a dominance that embraces others. In practical terms, when you have unconditional love, you fit in society rather than stand out.

We have shown in this book that there are many aspects of ourselves that we have to learn in life, such as responsibility, balance, understanding, self-esteem, creativity, and forgiveness. Anger can act as a pathway to the core of our soul, which is unconditional love. Each path that anger creates is necessary to lead us to the core of Love. When we are at our core, we are in union or yoga in the broadest sense of the term.

Because God by definition is infinite, there could be infinite pathways; we have only chosen to discuss a few in this book. If we choose to travel on only a few paths of anger that lead to love, but not other paths, we have not completed our life's lessons. It would be arrogant to say that one has learned all that life has to teach. The lessons in life, too, are infinite.

All paths of anger to love are important for our soul's journey. We need to travel on each path so that we become complete and whole. When we have completely healed ourselves, we can become a beacon of love, capable of radiating light from our core. The more pathways of anger we travel on, the brighter our light will be, and the more we will be able to heal and transform others.

There are infinite pathways of anger to love. All these pathways lead to unconditional love, the core of our soul. The more pathways we travel, the greater our love will be, and the more we will be able to radiate light in order to heal and transform others. Only by transforming ourselves first can we transform others. Anger is a gift for our soul.

16

A SUMMARY OF THE SPIRITUAL LESSONS OF ANGER

*A*s we have seen in this book, our feelings of anger are an opportunity for us to grow spiritually and become aware of where we need to heal ourselves. Each area of inner space that we need to heal is a lesson that we need to learn. Our anger guides us to these inner spaces so that ultimately we become beacons of love.

Unless we walk the different paths of anger toward our destination of love, we cannot make our anger go away permanently. Events that generate anger will show up in our lives over and over again in various forms and disguises until we learn what the Universe is trying to teach us. This has important implications for a popular approach to anger management through physical release, such as punching pillows and screaming in a closed room to "vent it out."

Physical release in this way might provide temporary relief, but it is not going to offer a long-run solution to removing the unpleasant feelings associated with anger. Sooner or later, another angry event will pop up because we have not dealt with its spiritual root cause. Until we learn the spiritual lessons contained in the seed of anger, events and situations that sprout anger will continue to appear and grow.

The purpose of this chapter is to summarize all the chapters in Part II so that you can have a snapshot view of the lesson or lessons that you may need to learn. One of the first questions that you need to ask yourself when you are angry is, "**What do I need to learn about myself?**" or "**What is this experience trying to teach**

me?" All of the lessons may not be applicable to you. You may need to learn one lesson or a combination of them. However, you alone can determine the answer to this. Do some quiet reflection and ask yourself what you need to learn from your anger.

- **Do I need to be more personally responsible?**

    The Universe is based on the law of cause and effect: You get in life what you give out. Internalize this basic law. Responsibility in this sense means releasing all blame. It also means that you have the ability to respond to any situation. Be creative in your responses rather than being reactive.

- **Do I need to love myself more?**

    How much you love yourself will determine how successful and happy you will be in your life. Remember that you are infinite and timeless. Stop victim behaviors and remove all beliefs that you may be unworthy in some way.

- **Do I need to release old, outdated beliefs that no longer serve me?**

    You may be addicted to external power or status rather than true authentic power, or you could be addicted to your role as a caregiver or worker. It could also be your race or nationality. Examine the false beliefs you hang on to and release them.

- **Do I need to have more prosperity consciousness?**

    In your true state you are an Ocean of Abundance. Think of yourself this way. Remove beliefs that stand in the way of this. True prosperity means that you have an abundance of comfort, health, money, joy, creative growth, and loving relationships.

- **Do I need to lead a more balanced lifestyle?**

    A balanced lifestyle means that you have physical, emotional, and spiritual harmony. It is a state of peace. If you are not peaceful most of the time, you are likely to be in a state of imbalance due to some inner addiction. Determine what these addictions are and release them.

- **Do I need to be more compassionate and understanding?**

  The opposite of understanding and compassion is judgment. Understanding occurs when you learn to be in the other person's shoes and see the world through their eyes. By the law of cause and effect, don't expect people to understand you until you know how to understand them.

- **Do I need to be more creative?**

  Creativity is using your mind to make your life and your environment better. To be creative you don't have to be a superstar musician (although you can certainly aspire to be one). It means that you should try to be better than you used to be in any area of your life. It could mean being a better parent, worker, cook, or gardener.

- **Do I need to be more focused on the present moment?**

  If you are worrying about the future or thinking about the past, then you are not living in the present moment. Your worry about the future is based on fear. Learn to develop trust in yourself by knowing that you are Love. Similarly, you can release the past through forgiveness.

- **Do I need to learn unconditional love?**

  When you are capable of sending love no matter what happens in your life, you have learned what unconditional love means. You are able to do this because you realize that you are contained in everything and everyone. Everyone and everything is Spirit in material disguise.

While understanding the spiritual lessons of anger is important, anger management is a multi-step process. The following, which are practical steps in managing anger, are also important for you to incorporate into your daily routine. We will discuss these in greater detail in Part III, "Practical Steps to Heal Anger."

- Positive self-talk and affirmations
- Mindful meditation

- Compassionate communication if one needs to express anger
- Forgiveness and letting go
- Healing anger through daily acts of kindness
- Healing anger by sleeping well
- Managing anger in children

$\mathscr{P}$ART III

Practical Steps to Heal Anger

17

HEALING ANGER THROUGH POSITIVE SELF-TALK AND AFFIRMATIONS

*B*y now you realize that what you think and say does have an effect on your physical health and your outer experience of life. Any statement that you say to yourself is an affirmation. In other words, it is self-talk. When you say something positive to yourself such as "I love myself," or "I am worthy," it becomes positive self-talk. One way to heal your anger is to repeatedly say aloud or think about positive statements. This will enable these thoughts to be ingrained into your subconscious and become beliefs.

Let us remind you that anger is a symptom of negative thought patterns. You may feel anger if you think negatively about someone (e.g., blame someone), or when your existing beliefs at the subconscious level are challenged. These negative thoughts associated with angry feelings can produce damaging chemicals in your body, which may lead to a host of diseases including cancer and heart disease. In Chapter 2, we noted, for example, that angry thoughts release catecholamines, which can lead to heart disease, a major killer.

Therefore, if negative thoughts can cause disease, positive thoughts should heal your body. There is sufficient scientific evidence that positive self-talk statements that are repeated can have a beneficial effect on your physical health. Researchers at the Harvard Medical School's Mind/Body Institute and similar institutions around the country routinely teach their patients to use positive self-talk to "think away" their stress-related illnesses. The term *cognitive restructuring* is used in these institutions to describe the process of reversing the negative thought patterns into positive ones.

Another term for how positive belief can have a beneficial effect on your health is the so-called *placebo effect.* A placebo is a sugar pill that is used in clinical trials. In the trial, patients are not told whether they are taking a sugar pill or a real pill with an active ingredient. Patients who are actually taking a sugar pill get better because they *believe* they are taking a real pill with an active ingredient. In other words, their belief produced the better health rather than the pill itself. Countless studies have confirmed the placebo effect.

In addition to the fact that positive self-talk will have a beneficial effect on your body, it will also have an effect on your outer experience of life, whether it is to do with relationships, your career, or finances. The reason for this is that you are also a part of the cosmic body. You are a part of Infinite Intelligence and are a cocreator of your life. This means that the law of cause and effect governs your life. What you repeatedly think or say will materialize as experience.

Words, which are expressed in sound, are actually more powerful than our thoughts because sound involves more condensed energy than thought. Sound is the bridge between the abstract world of thoughts and the concreteness of the material world. Saying affirmations loudly can, therefore, send a powerful message to the Universe, which will "boomerang back," or materialize your verbal expression. The following are affirmations that you may want to use to manage your anger.

"I AM HEALED"

Since the purpose of our anger is to teach us to become whole, i.e., to heal spiritually, this is a powerful affirmation to say. This is an all-encompassing affirmation because it says to the Universe that we want a comprehensive solution. Also, always use the present tense such as, "I *am* healed," rather than "I *will* be healed," because the former makes a stronger statement. While you say the affirmation, you also may want to visualize yourself as healed. This image, for example, might involve seeing yourself in a calm and peaceful state of mind in a tranquil setting as a mountain lake.

"I AM RESPONSIBLE"

Becoming 100 percent responsible for your life is a core approach to managing anger. Repeating this affirmation will signal the Universe that you want to see yourself as a cocreator of your life and do not want to impose blame on anyone or any situation. This is why this is an important and powerful affirmation. You can also supplement this affirmation with "I am One," indicating to the Universe that you do not see yourself as separate from anyone else, and therefore do not blame anyone. Visualize everyone, including your supposed "enemy" melting into the same ocean of pure space energy.

Never say an affirmation in negative terms such as, "I don't want to be angry." Since the Universe hears the word "angry," that is what will show up in your life. Always phrase affirmations in positive words, stating them in what you want rather than what you don't want. "I am peaceful" and "I am in harmony" are also affirmations you can use.

"I AM DIVINE"

Since your anger could be a symptom of low esteem, this is an important affirmation. If your mind says, "This doesn't make sense," refer to Figure 2 in Chapter 4 and convince your mind that you are, indeed, a part of the Divine. Once your mind sees the logic behind it, it will find it easier to believe and accept this is true. As you say this affirmation, you also might want to picture a radiant light coming out from your heart. As you visualize and repeat this affirmation, you will actually feel a warm glow in your heart.

In Part II, you saw that anger could be a symptom of low self-esteem or poverty consciousness. If this is the case, go back to Chapters 8 and 9 and take some affirmations listed in those sections and repeat them. Affirmations such as, "I love myself, I deserve the best" and "I am worthy" are examples especially for self-esteem.

By repeating your affirmations over and over, as often as you can, they will gradually become internalized. In other words, your subconscious mind will really start believing them to be true. When the truth of these is accepted, you will "materialize" these affirmations as experience because of the law of cause and effect. If you want to help a loved one manage their anger, you can also do affirmations on their behalf without them even knowing about it. In such cases you would say something along the lines of, "Jack is healed," or "Jack is divine." Since everyone literally occupies the same energy field, the impact on someone else can be profound and instantaneous.

Repeated positive self-talk and affirmations can have a powerful effect by changing your health and life experiences in general.

18

MEDITATION: LEARNING TO PAUSE AND STEP BACK

*O*ne of the most important aspects of anger management is to learn to pause and step back from reactive behavior. If we have angry feelings, it is wise not to act on our impulses either verbally or through physical action. Meditation is a method that can help you learn to pause and step back so that you can effectively express your anger.

What exactly is meditation? Meditation is simply a process by which you **pay whole-hearted attention to whatever you happen to be doing or not doing *now*.** This is the broadest definition of the term. It is a process of detached, yet focused attention. Because meditation by definition is focusing on now, the present moment, it teaches you not to be impulsive.

Meditation is about making yourself more aware or conscious of your thoughts, words, and actions. You can learn to become conscious of your thoughts and feelings when you learn to pay focused attention in a nonjudgmental way. Nonjudgment means you avoid thought patterns such as, "I don't like this," or "This is good or this is bad." These are mental labels as we mentioned before. Meditation is only one of the steps needed for comprehensive anger management. By itself, it will not "cure" or make our anger go away. However, it is an important tool that we can use to learn to stop and hold ourselves back. By doing so, we give ourselves an opportunity to really reflect on the meaning of our anger as well as to prevent impulsive behavior.

The following are some common meditations, which are simple and easy to implement in your daily life. These are the ones that have proved effective for us. We have divided these into active meditation and nonactive meditation for the sake of convenience.

Active meditation means being involved in an activity whereby you place your whole attention on that activity, without any external distractions. There is no struggle or exertion involved, and the purpose of it is not to get a result or outcome. Nonactive meditation involves doing nothing and usually involves setting aside formal time to be still and silent. Each type of meditation is discussed in turn.

ACTIVE MEDITATION

Eating Meditation

Each meal can be a meditation exercise provided you pay full attention to the taste, smell, and the act of drinking or chewing. Here are some meditation exercises to consider as the day goes by:

- *Morning Coffee Meditation:* If you drink coffee or tea in the morning (or whenever), try to relish those moments as you sip your beverage. Smell the aroma and look at the steam, if any is coming out. Observe the mug or cup that is holding the beverage. Are there designs that you never noticed before? Appreciate also the contour of the vessel. Avoid watching TV or the computer if you are in front of your desk. Doing so would only defeat the purpose of the meditation.
- *Lunch Meditation:* We often have a tuna sandwich for lunch with raw carrots on the side (if you don't like tuna, substitute this example with the lunch you normally eat). Slowly chew the sandwich and seep in the flavors of the tuna and

mayonnaise. Do the same for each bite instead of uncon- sciously gobbling it down. As you bite your carrots, hear the crunch of each bite and taste the juices coming out of the car- rot as you chew it slowly.

Do not judge the food as good or bad as you eat. If you are eating with others in a cafeteria, make it a point to minimize talking while eating, and finish your food first. Because it may be difficult not to talk, especially in the company of others, you may have to eat alone sometimes to practice this. Also, if you do eat alone, at your desk for instance, don't read your e-mails or catch up on other reading, as you might be tempted to.

Driving Meditation

We spend a lot of time in our cars and we can use this opportunity to practice paying attention to not only the process of driving itself (such as being aware that you are pressing the gas pedal, changing gears, or feeling your hand touch the steering wheel), but also absorbing the sights as they go by. The following illustrates an example of a driving meditation that I practiced recently.

It was a day when there was a winter storm in New Jersey, and my office closed early so that employees could go home safely before the weather worsened. What was typically a 15-minute drive home took almost 1½ hours. However, it was one of the most enjoyable and peaceful driving experiences I ever had.

While seeing cars stranded on the roadside and skidding in front of me, the natural inclination would have been to have fear- ful thoughts such as, "I hope I don't skid," or thoughts such as, "Oh, when am I going to get home?" Instead, my thoughts were along the lines, "What a spectacular sight." Indeed, I was thor- oughly enjoying the panorama of the usually brown and green landscape that had draped itself in a blanket of beautiful, fluffy white. The branches of trees gracefully bowed and drooped down, due to the weight of the snow and icicles, as if they were involved in an artistic dance.

Driving at the speed of 20 miles per hour, I could also hear the slow rhythmic drone of the windshield wipers as they cleared away the big fluffy snowflakes. I also put on some melodious piano music, which too, had a peaceful effect. When I came home I felt very relaxed and refreshed by watching such a beautiful performance by Mother Nature! Here is the bottom line: **It is not the "outside" event per se that causes distress, but rather *how you respond to it and your interpretation of it.***

Playing Meditation

If you have children, playing with them in a focused, yet relaxed way is also a form of meditation. As we often do, it might mean physically sitting down and playing with your small child and helping him or her build something with blocks, even if it is just for 15 minutes. It is important that the TV should not be turned on during these precious moments.

At other times, we often chase the kids around the house playing "monster." Both our children squeal with delight as mommy or daddy monster comes to "get them." Playing meditation is a great way to bond with your children. If you have been reactive to them, it is also an excellent way to make up to them. Giving attention to them in this way not only tells them you care about them, but also provides practice for your mind to be relaxed in a focused way.

Walking Meditation

On many warm, balmy, summer nights after the children have gone to bed, we often take a 15-minute walk outside. Taking deep breaths, stretching our arms and legs, smelling the fragrance of the flowers, and feeling the soft breeze go through our faces, is an excellent way to connect with nature in the night.

The idea of a walking meditation is not to get to a certain place, or increase your heart rate to a certain speed. The purpose of this type of meditation is to go with the flow of bodily movement. During the day at work, too, instead of spending a full hour eating lunch, you may want to set aside 15 minutes or so to walk around your facility, or outside it, if possible.

NONACTIVE MEDITATION

Doing-Nothing Meditation

Sitting still and not doing anything is one of the best meditation exercises you can do for yourself. Setting aside even 10 minutes is a great way to start, and can be gradually increased. When you are alone and silent, it is easier to hear the voice of your intuition, which is essentially the Divine, speaking to you. It is only during such moments of stillness that you can reflect on, and get answers to, the meaning of events that generate anger.

Since a critical part of anger management is trying to understand the lesson behind anger by asking the question, "What can I learn from this experience?", the best way to get the answer is when you are still and silent. It is during these periods of quiet that the Universe speaks through flashes of insight that "pop out" from the nonquantum realm.

If you refer back to Figure 2 in Chapter 4, being completely silent is the same thing as operating at the level of your soul. When you are at this level, you can view or witness your thoughts as they go by, as well as receive insight from the larger Soul, i.e., the Universe or Infinite Intelligence.

During these reflective moments, the idea is not to think or get answers by analyzing a problem, but simply to let your thoughts come in and out in a natural way, watching them as they do so. This watching or detached viewing is the process of "stepping back" as we mentioned earlier. By watching your thoughts, you begin to understand how your mind operates and you learn to become more conscious and aware.

Repetitive Word Meditation

Repeating a word over and over such as God, Yahweh, Allah, or Love (whatever one suits you), and focusing on those words in a concentrated way for even 5 minutes, can have a profound influence on calming the mind. A calm mind is the same thing as a mind that does not produce too many thoughts. Although thoughts will come in and out while you meditate, **the space between the thoughts** will increase the more you meditate. That's why we recommend at least 10 minutes. If you can increase it to 20 minutes per session, twice a day, that is even better.

The space between your thoughts is the same thing as soul or spirit as depicted in Figure 2 in Chapter 4. In other words, as you calm your mind, you are making more room for your individual soul and its ability to get access to the larger Soul, i.e., Pure Spirit. Getting access to your soul is the same thing as becoming detached from your mind and body, which in turn, will enable you to become less reactive. By viewing your mind and body from the position of your soul, you are learning how to pause and step back.

This kind of word meditation is essentially a repeated affirmation along the lines discussed earlier. However, you are doing this affirmation in a more focused way. Since the repetitive word is an affirmation, and what you say will materialize as experience, it is wise not to use words that have a negative meaning as we discussed in the last chapter on positive self-talk.

Here are the few simple steps that you need to do to practice this meditation. It is short, quick, and energizing.

- Sit comfortably in a quiet place where there are no distractions.
- Close your eyes and breathe deeply and slowly for a minute or so.

- Repeat any one word described previously, over and over for 10 minutes, focusing only on that word.
- Open your eyes and sit quietly for a few minutes after you have finished (you will feel very airy and "light").

A number of studies have also shown that this kind of meditation lowers the heart rate, blood pressure, and the respiration rate. All of these different effects have lifelong health advantages by slowing the aging process. Some of these studies have shown that for people meditating for more than 5 years, their biological age (as measured by their blood pressure, heart rate, vision, and hearing abilities) was 12 years younger than their chronological age (so, for example, if someone is 50 years old, their physical health is like someone who is 38 years old).

Meditation also changes our brain wave frequencies to make them into *theta* waves. Studies have shown that when our brains are in the theta state, we are most creative and insightful. This makes sense from what we discussed before. Our creativity comes from the realm of our souls. When we access our souls through meditation, we literally create more open space in our minds by reducing our "mental chatter," which in turn allows creative thoughts to enter. The bottom line is this: In addition to helping you responsibly express your anger, repetitive word meditation has a host of other health benefits, which provides compelling reasons to take it up.

Breathing Meditation

The idea of a breathing meditation is to focus on your breath as you inhale and exhale. Once again the purpose is to train you to become conscious. If you've never tried a breathing meditation, observing yourself breathing in and out 10 times might be a good start.

Inhale through your nose and fill your lungs with a deep breath. Hold your breath for 10 seconds and then slowly exhale. Focus on your breath as you do this exercise. If your mind gets distracted or wanders off, focus again on your breath. Sitting in a comfortable position will assist you in this nonactive activity.

Aside from helping you to become conscious and aware, this kind of breathing meditation helps relieve and prevent stress. One reason we are often angry is because we are stressed out and out of balance. In fact, when you are stressed, your breathing is rapid and shallow. An additional benefit of this meditation is that your lung capacity will increase, which will enable it to supply more oxygen to all the cells in your body. As your body gets more oxygen on a regular basis (assuming you practice this meditation regularly), you will also feel more energized.

Prayer Meditation

Our formal prayers, whether they are in a mosque, church, synagogue, or at home can also be a great form of meditation, provided we are focusing on the act of praying, making sure that our minds don't wander off. Instead of mechanically saying or doing our prayers, the idea is to focus on every aspect of the prayer in a whole-hearted way.

We would like to end this chapter by noting that the characteristics of meditation, i.e., focused attention, present moment awareness, and nonjudgment can encompass all aspects of our lives. As we become more conscious of everything we do or do not do, we are automatically becoming more conscious of our thoughts and beliefs. As this process happens, we will be able to respond creatively to our anger and our life in general.

Mindful meditation is focused attention on the "now." It can help you learn to step back and pause, allowing you to become less reactive and more proactive.

19

COMPASSIONATE COMMUNICATION:

How to Give Feedback When You Are Angry

*A*key part of anger management is compassionate communication. It is important to express your feelings and your point of view in a nonattacking way, even if you are right and they are wrong. Communicating to another person for a perceived injustice may not always be necessary, especially if you have learned the spiritual lesson behind the angry event.

Sometimes, however, it may be important to communicate with another person so our needs can be met without harming them. There are basically two ways you can communicate: either verbally or by writing. You can also do a combination of the two. Let us discuss each in turn.

VERBAL COMMUNICATION

As a general principle, your goal for the communication is *dialogue* and not simply a one-way lecture. Further, your goal is to achieve a sense of peace at the end of the conversation by having a better understanding of the person and the situation. If you are going to give negative feedback (or any feedback when you are angry), here are the steps that you need to take that have been proven to be effective for us:

1. **Don't give feedback in the heat of the moment.** Cool down first, and give yourself plenty of time to think about

what you are going to say—it could be hours or days. *Visualize* a peaceful outcome of your conversation.

2. **Arrange for a meeting when both of you have plenty of time** to discuss the issue. Before starting the conversation, make eye contact with the person and *smile.* There are studies that show that the act of smiling itself reduces tension. Have a totally open mind and avoid judging or blaming thoughts. Have a physical posture that suggests openness, such as arms relaxing on both sides of a chair; avoid folding your arms or crossing your legs.

3. When starting the conversation, you may begin with, "How are things going?" **Really *listen* for what the other person has to say by repeating or playing back what he or she has said.** Often a perceived injustice and the anger it generates occurs because we do not know where the other person is coming from. Seek to understand the other person by asking questions rather than trying to have him or her become the way you think they should be. Your goal is to understand how he or she thinks and approaches issues and problems. Refer to Chapter 14 for ideas on mindful listening.

4. Before going to the topic immediately, **praise** that person. **Why? It will soften any criticism you are going to give.** Something along the lines such as "Jack, you are a wonderful person" is fine. You can also be specific in praising someone's qualities or specific things that they recently did.

5. Once you feel you have established a climate of friendly rapport where both of you appear to be comfortable, you might **say something along the lines of, "I would like to discuss something with you."** Describe the situation in concise terms using facts rather than interpretations. Focus on what the person has done, not on who they are.

6. Go on to the issue you want to discuss, **starting with, "I feel . . ." Avoid saying, "*You* did this to me."** Remember,

you are the one who is experiencing the angry feelings and the other person is simply the "trigger." Further, there is no such thing as blame from a spiritual standpoint.

7. Say clearly what you want, but **avoid the word "but" and use "and" instead.** For example, "I feel you are an intelligent person *and* I think your work could improve" is a better phrase than "I feel you are an intelligent person *but* I think your work could improve." The problem with "but" indicates that there is something wrong that needs to be fixed. Even if there is a real problem, using the word "and" is softer and more kind.

8. Depending on what the issue is, **focus on solutions and allow the other person to respond.** Use statements such as, "How would you prefer to handle this?", "What are your thoughts?", or "Here's is my request."

9. Always **let the other person save face especially if they are the "culprit."** No one wants to be put in the corner. When they are in this situation, they may become defensive and it makes them feel small. You don't want to make anyone feel small or belittle them in any way. Remember, you occupy the same energy field as everyone else.

10. **Close the conversation with a positive note such as, "It was good talking with you.** I have a better understanding of the situation." Talk about the positive things that both of you have learned from this experience.

While you are communicating you should be vocally aware regarding the *tone* of voice you are going to use. The best approach of course is to be even-toned. However, at times it may be necessary to raise your voice to get the point across, especially if you have given gentle feedback before and it hasn't worked.

The approach that we have just outlined is applicable to anyone, whether it is your spouse, a coworker, or a boss. The bottom line is: After both of you have had a conversation, you want to feel emotionally unburdened by having the blocks of resentment dissolved, and you want to feel at peace.

WRITTEN COMMUNICATION

Since a large part of our written communication these days is through e-mail, let us discuss anger communication through this method first. Generally speaking, we tend to avoid e-mail when we sense there is scope for misunderstanding for the following reasons:

- The same words may have different meanings for different people.
- Communicators can have different assumptions.
- Words may be inadequate to express difficult concepts or ideas.
- There can be lack of privacy, as e-mail can be "copied" or "forwarded" to other persons.
- You cannot see facial expressions or hear the tone of voice, so you don't know whether something is being said in a raised voice or not. Therefore, there is scope for misinterpretation.
- You may become stressed out in front of the computer waiting for the other person to respond.

When you sense that an e-mail could lead to a potentially tense situation, especially during work, the best way to "nip it in the bud" is to meet the person physically if you can. If you can't do that, give them a phone call or arrange a teleconference.

There are clear trends that the western economies are gradually becoming "virtual economies." This means that people tend to work more in geographically dispersed areas (such as working from home), instead of working in one central office location. This implies that people will see less of each other and tend to communicate electronically. This obviously raises the issue that there can be increased scope for misunderstanding and miscommunication. Sometimes, however, letter writing may be a better initial vehicle than verbal communication, especially if you want the other person to "digest" and really think over the issues that you want to address. If you do write a letter, either electronically or by hardcopy, here are some guidelines to follow:

1. Follow the steps in this chapter found in the section on "Verbal Communication," such as praising a person first; then **begin with "I" statements.**
2. **Review the letter a few days later** when you are calmer and can think in a detached way.
3. If possible, **let a close friend or spouse review the letter to give objective feedback** regarding choice of words and phrases. A second pair of eyes can easily spot any hostility that you may not be aware of.
4. Finally, **use your feelings as a guide to decide if the letter feels "right."** If you feel anguish and turmoil, then it is not a "right" letter. If, on the other hand, you feel peaceful, it is a "right" letter. It is as simple as that.

The steps that we have outlined are guidelines regarding how to communicate and give feedback. Depending on the situation involved, you have to tailor it to meet your needs.

Compassionate communication means asserting your needs without harming others. It is a process of having a dialogue with someone when you show understanding and empathy.

20

LETTING GO AND FORGIVING

*A*s we noted in Chapter 19, a key process of anger management is forgiveness of the past. This is especially important when it is no longer possible to communicate with the person (or persons) in question as they may have physically left your life. It is impossible to heal ourselves unless we have forgiven our past and the resentments that we store within us. We may have forgotten about these incidents, but nevertheless the negative energy is still inside us and needs to be released.

If you don't release your resentments, the Universe will either bring forth incidents that generate anger or cause the blocked energy to manifest itself as physical disease. One of the best analogies we can give you so that you realize the importance of releasing your past is that of a plant which has dead branches.

As gardeners know, a plant will be stunted in growth unless the dead branches are cut off. The reason for this is that most of the energies of a plant go to revive the dead branches because the plant "thinks" that those branches are still alive; consequently this takes away energy from the new shoots, hence preventing growth.

Like a plant with dead branches it is impossible to grow spiritually unless we get rid of our resentments. Holding on to resentments can consume an enormous amount of energy. Like a plant we may assume that our memories are "real" or "alive"; however, for all practical purposes they have no real life of their own. If you recall from Chapter 3, our purpose in life is to realize we are divine. This realization can only happen if we make inner room for ourselves to grow spiritually by cutting the dead branches of our resentments and perceived past hurts.

Resentments are in fact memories. And what is a memory? A memory is simply a fixed image or picture that you have in your mind. A memory based on resentment is an image that is stored in your mind that shows that someone has wronged you (or you have wronged yourself).

A memory is a fixed image with no life of its own, just like a painting or photograph. Forgiveness means that you simply "erase" each negative image and leave yourself with a clean memory slate. You may then go one step further and "draw" a positive picture on each memory slate that you have cleaned with an affirmation. Here is an exercise that can help you release your past.

- **Go back in time to when you were 16 or 17 years of age.** Start at that age and remember any angry or resentful situation that caused you pain. Think of each situation as a memory picture. Your goal is to erase each negative picture from your energy system.
- **For each negative memory, write out the incident and what pained you.** Write this on a paper or an erasable board. You may also want to draw an angry face. A picture may be worth a thousand words and will be more memorable. After drawing the picture or writing, *cross out the whole page and throw it away.*
- **On another clean paper, write statements such as "I forgive you," or "I forgive myself,"** depending on what the event was. As you write these statements, say them aloud too. Use a golden or yellow pen, which will enable you to visualize the glow and radiance from these "replacement" memory pictures. Draw a happy smiling face next to these statements.
- **Do this process for every year that you can remember.** If any one particular year does not have any negative incident, go on to the next year. Simply repeat the process until you have finished your entire lifespan.

You can also refer back to Figure 2 in Chapter 4 and imagine yourself as a part of Infinite Intelligence. You can say to yourself, " I am one with Infinite Intelligence. The same energy that is in the other person is the same energy that is in me." This way you can convince your ego that you are not separate from the person who is causing you the pain.

A key aspect of forgiveness is that although we release blame, it is important that we do not forget the incident. As we discussed in Part II, one of the major purposes of our anger is to teach us about ourselves so that we can heal. By understanding the lesson and what it has taught us, we will not experience any future negative experience dealing with that particular lesson.

While we have discussed how resentment toward someone else points to the need for us to cultivate the qualities of forgiveness and mercy, the same can be said when we have anger that is directed towards ourselves. Often, we are angry with ourselves because we have made mistakes in the past.

Any mistake should be viewed as a learning opportunity for our spiritual growth. If we label the experience as a mistake, then it will remain as a mistake and so will our attached anger. If, however, we label it as a learning opportunity, we are free to release the blame on ourselves. When we release blame, we free our spirits. Our spirit is then free to walk on the path of its full potentiality.

Forgiveness means replacing a negative memory picture of someone with a positive one. It is a process of releasing the past. When we do this, we make room for our spiritual growth.

21

HEALING ANGER THROUGH
DAILY ACTS OF KINDNESS

*A*nger is a symptom of too much preoccupation with our own life. It occurs because we are concerned with ego needs of "I," "me," and "mine." One practical way to heal anger is to focus on others with daily acts of kindness and generosity. A number of studies have also shown that when you are altruistic, you will boost your immune system and release healing chemicals known as endorphins.

Other studies have even gone further to document that the risk of death is affected when one practices helping others. One study found that men who volunteered in a community were two-and-a-half times more likely to live longer than those who did not volunteer. You don't have to be Mother Theresa to do this. You can practice kindness and generosity even in the most ordinary of days. Here are some examples:

- Send a thank you note or e-mail acknowledging someone's contribution to good work. Don't take anyone for granted.
- Wipe the counter surrounding the coffee station at work to make it clean for the next person.
- Smile as often as you can. Smile at your loved ones when you come home. Smile at people at work, including the janitor; practice smiling in front of the mirror until it becomes automatic.

- Let someone in traffic go before you.
- Give someone credit openly in public for good work they have done.
- Give a compliment to someone on their dress or how they look.
- Be kind to yourself by being open to receiving compliments. Don't say in response, "It was nothing," or "Don't mention it." Simply say, "Thank you."
- Don't squash an insect or spider that is in your house. Simply pick it up with a paper towel and take it outside. (Of course if there are many insects, you may have to use "pest control." You might think about the symbolic significance of too many bugs in your house, though, if this is the case.)
- Hold open the door for someone if they are just behind you or if their arms are full.

As you practice these daily acts of kindness you will find that you are more connected to others, which in turn will help develop within you a stronger sense of compassion. Additionally, you will feel more relaxed and better about yourself. In other words, your prosperity consciousness will expand in the broadest sense of the term.

Practicing daily acts of kindness will open your heart and allow your anger to heal. Allowing more generosity into your life will remove the focus off yourself, which is the basis of anger.

22

HEALING ANGER
BY SLEEPING WELL

*T*here is a direct relationship between how well you sleep and your threshold for irritation and anger. As we mentioned in various chapters of Part II, if you cannot sleep well whether it is because of insomnia or other sleep disorders, you will feel fatigued during the day and have little energy. As a result, there is a strong likelihood that you will feel irritated and angry even at the demands of a normal routine. Lack of sleep due to sleep disorders is also related to a host of illnesses such as heart disease, depression, a weakened immune system, risk of infections, heartburn, and impotence.[1]

Although underlying sleep disorders can make you irritable and angry, you can also start a cycle of disturbed and insufficient sleep by harboring resentment and anger. A number of studies have confirmed that chronic insomnia is often due to suppressed anger. Refer to Chapter 2 for a summary of these studies. Depression is a common reason for sleep disturbance. Note that depression is anger turned inwards. Any resentment can cause a downward spiral of insufficient sleep. The more anger you experience during the day, the more sleep difficulties you will face at night.

---

[1]Please visit our Web site, www.SleepHealthDoc.com, to get your free special report on how to get quality sleep for good health.

As the vicious cycle of poor sleep intensifies, you may start believing that you can never get enough sleep. Typical self-talk like, "I will never be able to sleep again," "I will remain awake at night," or "I am unable to function during the day because I can't sleep at night," are examples. As seen in many insomnia patients, negative beliefs actually make things worse because the placebo effect is working in reverse. Refer to Chapter 17 to refresh your memory of how self-talk and the placebo effect work. The bottom line is that the belief itself will have a material impact on your body.

One way to reverse the vicious cycle of negative beliefs is to change the negative self-talk into positive self-talk. Examples might be:

- **I get sufficient sleep at night.**
- **I enjoy sleeping.**
- **I fall asleep quickly and stay asleep.**
- **I am deeply rested in sleep.**
- **My sleep health is excellent.**

Repeating these statements over and over, day and night will imprint your subconscious with these new beliefs. Through the placebo effect, you will be able to see an improvement in your sleep.

Society has generally downplayed the importance of sleep, despite the fact that we spend almost one-third of our time in this activity. One reason for this is that little sleep medicine research was done until 20 years ago.

This lack of knowledge is also responsible for the fact that only about 2 to 3 hours of sleep medicine is taught to medical students in their 4 years of medical school training. From a practical standpoint, therefore, your average primary care physician, due to no fault of his own, is not aware of the need to ask you about your sleep health. Because of this, **almost 95 percent of sleep disorders go undiagnosed.** The health consequences of this lack of awareness can be deadly. Since you are armed with this knowledge now, it behooves you that you be more proactive about your sleep health.

If you are frequently irritable and you cannot find any other cause for this, it may be wise to ask yourself if you are getting sufficient sleep. The average person needs about 8 hours a day, but the amount can vary from 6 hours to 10 hours.

The big test of good sleep health is whether you feel fully alert during the day. It is abnormal to feel sleepy during the day. If you don't feel alert, it may be a sign that you are not getting enough sleep or that you may have a sleep disorder. If the sleep disorder is insomnia, one common reason for this is unnecessary stress due to an imbalanced lifestyle. We mentioned in Chapter 11 that you may be able to remove some of the stress in your life by resetting your priorities.

Another common sleep disorder is sleep apnea. In addition to symptoms of irritability and anger during the day, other symptoms include heavy snoring during the night and being overweight. However, you don't have to be overweight to have sleep apnea.

With sleep apnea, airflow is obstructed while you sleep. This happens because tissue in your throat relaxes during sleep. As airflow is obstructed, you don't get oxygen. As often as every 30 seconds, therefore, you may be aroused by your brain to restart breathing. This process fragments sleep and causes excessive daytime tiredness. In many cases, you may not be aware of the fact that you were awakened by your brain hundreds of times in the course of the night.

If you snore at night and are sleepy and irritable during the day, you may have to take a sleep test to determine whether you have sleep apnea. Snoring, sleepiness during the day, and being overweight are common symptoms of sleep apnea. Don't ignore these symptoms because recent studies have shown that sleep apnea is related to heart disease, the number one killer in our society. In order to learn more about sleep disorders and how you can achieve a good night's rest, please visit our Web site at www.SleepHealthDoc.com.

Your sleep health is a vital part of your overall health. Your anger can be both a symptom and a cause of poor sleep patterns.

23

MANAGING ANGER IN CHILDREN

If you have children who are angry, you will need to take personal responsibility for their situation. Because of the law of cause and effect, your children will mirror you. If you are reactive, resentful, or frequently expressing anger in an aggressive way, these are qualities they will also display.

Refer to Chapter 7 on "Anger as a Pathway to Responsibility," and determine whether you are behaving in a responsible way with your children. As we discussed in that chapter, when we took more personal responsibility in our lives, our daughter became a less angry child. If you have older children who have left the nest, you may need to practice compassionate communication, as described earlier.

One of the reasons for the initial cycle of anger between our daughter and us was due to the birth of our son. The anger Rania faced initially was induced by jealousy. Much of the reactivity we displayed towards Rania happened after she fought with her brother or hit him. In addition to taking more personal responsibility, we used some of the following strategies that helped Rania manage her anger.

DRAWING ANGER OUT

Quite literally, a child can draw anger in the form of art. As our daughter loves to draw and color, we found that when she was

4 years old, she was drawing people with angry faces. These faces had raised eyebrows and pouty lips. Once she drew a highly creative picture of herself with all four limbs having an angry face, symbolizing her wanting to hit and kick her brother. This is one kind of drawing that we encouraged.

As children need to express their anger, this is a harmless way for them to vent it. Drawing is a powerful energy release because feelings are being released physically. We should not encourage our children to suppress their anger. Suppressed anger is the same thing as resentment, which can materialize later as disease when the child becomes an adult, or it could be expressed as reactivity. It is our responsibility that our grandchildren and great-grandchildren do not pass on resentment from generation to generation in a vicious chain.

LAUGHING AND CHASING ANGER OUT

Often our children end up in a scuffle over a toy, with one snatching it from the other. The older one usually does this and the younger one ends up crying. Instead of always giving the older one time out, we often dissipate the tense situation and stop the fighting with tickling them. The fighting immediately stops and turns into laughter. Another strategy we have used to distract them from fights is by playfully chasing them. As we mentioned in Chapter 18 on meditation, playing with your children in a focused yet relaxed way is a form of "playing meditation."

LOVE ANGER OUT

Love, of course, is the best antidote to dealing with jealousy-induced anger in a child. Parents really have to go out of their way to make a jealous child feel not neglected. Often we hug and kiss the older child in front of the younger one. While this is a normal thing that all parents should do, being extra affectionate and more conscious of the need to do this is very important.

We also have one-to-one sessions with our daughter, whereby each of us asks questions about her daily activities and listens to her with focused attention. We call these "discussion times" and they typically last 15 to 20 minutes. Typical questions involve what she did at school, what her teachers or her friends said, or with whom she played with.

This kind of "asking and listening" meditation demonstrates to the child that you really care. It is also a good way to strengthen the spiritual bond between a parent and child. Our daughter likes these sessions so much that when we have finished asking questions, she says, "Why aren't you asking more questions?"

In the end, parents have to make appropriate judgments and see which approach works best in any given situation. Obviously, if some of these gentler approaches don't work, traditional time out sessions may be necessary. One has to certainly balance freedom and love with discipline.

We would like to point out that one thing we have **not** consciously sought to do is to label our children with words such as "bad." This kind of labeling not only teaches them to be judgmental, but could also leave a deep psychological scar on them. During time out sessions we might say, "We love you and this kind of behavior is not allowed in this family," instead of saying, "You're bad."

Even at a young age, it is possible to teach children about the law of cause and effect, i.e., "As you sow, so shall you reap." It might make them see the connection between what they say and do and how it might come back as another experience. One time, for instance, our daughter stuck her tongue out to her little brother. That very afternoon, when she went to play with her friend, her friend did exactly what she had done to her brother. Upset, she complained to us. Our reply was "Because you did not behave nicely with your brother, your friend did not behave nicely with you."

Making our children conscious at an early age of their actions amounts to training them to be responsible. While pointing out the boomerang impact of their negative acts may be done once in a while, it is 10 times more important to specifically point out their good behaviors and praise them lavishly for every improvement they make. In other words, catch them at doing something right.

With a combination of spiritually working through our own anger as well as making a conscious effort to provide extra love and attention to our daughter, there have been great improvements in Rania's behavior towards her brother. Not surprisingly, we can also see the big transformation in her art as well. In fact, she has now stopped drawing angry faces and is always drawing figures with bright smiling faces.

If your children are resentful or are expressing anger in aggressive ways, you need to take personal responsibility as a first step. Their anger may simply be a symptom that you have to go out of your way to provide extra love, care, and attention to them.

Appendix

ANGER MANAGEMENT CHECKLIST: WHAT TO DO WHEN YOU ARE ANGRY

*I*n this section we are going to give you a checklist of what to do when you are angry. It is a snapshot overview of all the principles we discussed in this book.

1. Ask yourself, **"What is my anger teaching me about myself?"** or "What do I need to learn?" Asking the right questions will give you the right answers. The "right" answer may be that you need to learn compassion, understanding, self-love, or any of the qualities discussed in Part II. If you think you've found the spiritual answer, you may not always need to express your anger verbally. If, however, you feel you do, then you need to ask the following question also.

2. **If I need to express my anger, what is the best way to do so?**
   a. *Set the stage using affirmations.* Visualize that you want a peaceful outcome with the person you want to communicate with. Then, repeat affirmations such as "I am love," or "I am divine," indicating your oneness with the person with whom you are going to communicate.
   b. *Meditate.* Meditation is the process of paying attention to what you are doing or not doing now. It is a process where you are conscious of your thoughts, words, and actions. Learning to become conscious will enable you to carefully choose your thoughts, words, and your

voice tone as you express your anger. In other words, you will learn to pause and step back, and consequently not be reactive. Mindful meditation should be a lifelong process integrated into your daily activities.

c. *Communicate compassionately.* The following are steps that you need to take to communicate your anger compassionately to another person:

- *Smile* and really *listen* to what the other person has to say.
- *Praise* the other person.
- Start the conversation with *"I"* statements rather than "You" statements
- *Communicate* your needs.
- Close the conversation with a *positive* note.

3. **What if the person has left my life so that I cannot express my anger to him or her?** In this case, forgiveness is the answer. To forgive means that we erase a negative memory picture of someone with a positive one. It is important that you learn to forgive that person, but not forget the spiritual lesson that was behind the experience.

4. **Integrate daily acts of kindness into your life.** You will be less angry or irritable in your life if you can practice more generosity in your daily life. Generosity will open your heart. Further, you will get more back because of the law of cause and effect.

5. **Examine whether you are sleeping well as this could be a cause of your anger.** Lack of sleep may make you angry during the day. This may be because you do not have a balanced lifestyle or it could be because you have a sleep disorder. Pay attention to your sleep health and consult your physician if necessary.[1]

---

[1]Please visit our Web site, www.SleepHealthDoc.com, to get your free special report on how to get quality sleep for good health.

AFTERWORD

$\mathcal{W}$e hope this book has given you a window to peer into your soul. The process of writing this book has certainly helped us to see the light within our own souls. It would be arrogant, however, to declare that we have "arrived" and are enlightened.

Enlightenment is a process and not a destination. As a general principle, whenever we think we have "arrived," there will always be a new challenge so that we get stretched towards greater divinity.

The purpose of our lives is to find the light within our own souls and to realize that we are bathed in the same One Light. Without darkness first, however, we cannot find light. Our feelings in general, and our anger in particular, are like guides with lanterns who lead us out of our tunnels of darkness into the open daylight of our brilliance.

Sometimes these lanterns glow softly, and sometimes they burn with a rage. The longer the journey, the greater is the rage. However, without the light that emanates from the fire of our rage, we cannot see our way through. When we finally arrive at the end of the tunnel and see our brilliance, we are forced to realize that light and darkness are two halves of the same one whole.

We have shown in this book that God speaks to us in symbols. This symbolic language is expressed as a paradox. In fact, paradox *is* the language of the Divine. What seems "small" is often "large."

What seems "good" is often "bad." What is a "disaster" is often a "blessing." Our feelings and our anger can help us to crack the code of this symbolic language. Cracking the code is not sufficient, though, because we also have to understand the hidden meanings behind the message. We can only understand these messages if we are willing to listen to our intuition, which is the voice of our souls.

Getting in touch with our intuition means that we need to become conscious and aware of what is happening around us and within us, moment by moment. It means by definition that our entire lives should be a meditation. It means that in a contemporary world where we have to maintain jobs and families, we need to make our so-called "ordinary" moments extra-ordinary. From a spiritual standpoint there is no such thing as an ordinary moment, because God is everywhere, in everyone, and in everything.

The "promised land" of peace of mind is here and now. Our spiritual journey is a process of realization that we do not need to go anywhere or acquire anything to achieve this state of peace we long for. This realization can only happen by becoming conscious that we are not separated from anyone or anything, but rather we are in reality one and whole. The notion that we are omnipresent, one, and whole has been a central theme of this book. We hope this book has brought more awareness to you of the need to become conscious of your wholeness, as well as an awareness of how anger can be a pathway toward this goal.

REFERENCES

Bach, David. *Smart Women Become Rich.* New York: Broadway, 1999.

Bonnet, M. H., and D. L. Arand. 1997. "Physiological Activation in Patients with Sleep State Misperception." *Psychosomatic Medicine* 59: 533–540.

Brody, C. L., D. A. F. Haaga, L. Kirk, and A. Solomon. 1999. "Experiences of Anger in People Who Have Recovered from Depression and Never-Depressed People." *Journal of Nervous and Mental Disease* 187: 400–405.

Chopra, Deepak. *Ageless Body, Timeless Mind.* New York: Harmony Books, 1993.

Chopra, Deepak. *How to Know God.* New York: Three Rivers Press, 2001.

Chopra, Deepak. *Perfect Health.* New York: Harmony Books, 1991.

Coursey, R. D., M. Buchsbaum, and B. L. Frankel. 1975. "Personality Measures and Evoked Responses in Chronic Insomniacs." *Journal of Abnormal Psychology* 84(3): 239–249.

Domar, Alice, and Henry Dehrer. *Self-Nurture.* New York: Penguin Books, 2000.

Dyer, Wayne. *Your Sacred Self.* New York: HarperCollins, 1995.

Everson, S. A., G. Kaplan, D. E. Goldberg, T. A. Lakka, J. Sivenius, and J. T. Salonen. 1999. *Stroke* 30: 523–528.

Ford, Debbie. *The Dark Side of the Light Chasers.* New York: Riverhead Books, 1998.

Freedman, R. R., and H. L. Sattler. 1982. "Physiological and Psychological Factors in Sleep-Onset Insomnia." *Journal of Abnormal Psychology* 91(5): 380–389.

Friedman, Howard S. 1987. "Possible Links Between Personality and Disease."*American Psychologist,* 540–555.

Gawain, Shakti. *Creative Visualization.* Novato: New World Library, 1995.

Goleman, Daniel. *Working with Emotional Intelligence.* New York: Bantam Books, 1998.

Gross, James. 1989. "Emotional Expression in Cancer Onset and Progression." *Social Science Medicine* 28(12): 1239–1248.

Grossarth-Maticek, R., J. Bastiaans, D. T. Kanazir. 1985. "Psychosocial Factors as Strong Predictors of Mortality from Cancer, Ischaemic Heart Disease, and Stroke: The Yugoslav Prospective Study." *Journal of Psychosomatic Research* 29(2): 167–176.

Hay, Louise. *The Power Is Within You.* Carlsbad, CA: Hay House, 1992.

Hill, Napoleon. *Think and Grow Rich.* New York: Fawcett Crest Books, 1960.

Jack, D. C., and D. Dill. 1992. "Silencing the Self Scale: Schemas of Intimacy Associated with Depression in Women." *Psychology of Women Quarterly* 16: 97–106.

Jacobs, Gregg D. *Say Good Night to Insomnia.* New York: Owl Books, 1998.

Kabat-Zinn, Jon. *Wherever You Go, There You Are.* New York: Hyperion, 1995.

Kales, A., A. B. Caldwell, T. A. Preston, S. Healey, and J. D. Kales. 1996. "Personality Patterns in Insomnia: Theoretical Implications." *Archives of General Psychiatry* 33: 1128–1134.

Kubzansky, L. D., and I. Kawachi. 2000. "Going to the Heart of the Matter: Do Negative Emotions Cause Coronary Heart Disease?" *Journal of Psychosomatic Research* 48: 323–337.

Lehrer, Paul. 1998. "Emotionally Triggered Asthma: A Review of Research Literature and Some Hypotheses for Self-Regulation Therapies." *Applied Psychophysiology and Biofeedback* 23(1): 13–41.

Lehrer, P. M., S. Isenberg, and S. M. Hochron. 1993. "Asthma and Emotion: A Review." *Journal of Asthma* 30(1): 5–21.

McDermott, M. R., J. M. C. Ramsay, and C. Bray. 2001. "Components of the Anger-Hostility Complex as Risk Factors for Coronary Artery Disease Severity: A Multi-Measure Study." *Journal of Health Psychology* 6(3): 309–319.

Miller, T. Q., T. W. Smith, C. W. Turner, M. L. Guijarro, and A. J. Hallet. 1996. "A Meta-Analytic Review of Research on Hostility and Physical Health." *Psychological Bulletin* 119(2): 322–348.

Morris, T., S. Greer, K. W. Pettingale., and M. Watson. 1981. "Patterns of Anger and Their Psychological Correlates in Women with Breast Cancer." *Journal of Psychosomatic Research* 25(2): 111–117.

Muller, J. E., P. G. Kaufman, R. V. Luepker, M. L. Weisfeldt, P. C. Deedwania, and J. T. Willerson. 1997. "Mechanisms Precipitating Acute Cardiac Events: Review and Recommendations of an NHLBI Workshop." *Circulation* 96: 3233–3239.

Orman, Suze. *The Courage to Be Rich.* New York: Riverhead Books, 1999.

Riley, W. T., F. A. Treiber, and M. G. Woods. 1989. "Anger and Hostility in Depression." *The Journal of Nervous and Mental Diseases* 177(11): 668–674.

Sarafino, E. P., M. E. Peterson, and E. L. Murphy. 1998. "Age and the Impacts of Triggers in Childhood Asthma." *Journal of Asthma* 35(2): 213–217.

Siegel, Bernie. *Love, Medicine, and Miracles.* New York: Harper Collins, 1986.

Spielberger, C. D., G. Jacobs, S. Russell, and R. S. Crane. 1983. "Assessment of Anger: The Strait-Trait Anger Scale." In *Advances in Personality Assessment,* vol. 2. eds. J. N. Butcher and C. D. Spielberger. Hillsdale, NJ: Lawrence Erlbaum Associates, 161–189.

Tal, A., and D. Miklich. 1976. "Emotionally Induced Decreases in Pulmonary Flow Rates in Asthmatic Children." *Psychosomatic Medicine* 38(3): 190–200.

Temoshok, Lydia. 1987. "Personality, Coping Style, Emotion, and Cancer: Towards an Integrative Model." *Cancer Surveys* 6(3): 546–567.

Van Der Ploeg, H. M., W. C. Kliejn, J. Mook, M. Van Donge, A. M. J. Pieters, and J. H. Leer. 1989. "Rationality and Antiemotionality as a Risk Factor for Cancer: Concept Differentiation." *Journal of Psychosomatic Research* 33(2): 217–225.

Waters, F. W., S. G. Adams, P. Binks, and P. Varnado. 1993. "Attention, Stress, and Negative Emotion in Persistent Sleep-Onset and Sleep-Maintenance Insomnia." *Sleep* 16(2): 28–136.

Williams, J. E., C. C. Paton, I. C. Siegler, M. L. Eigenbrodt, F. J. Nieto, and H. A. Tyroler. 2000. "Anger Proneness Predicts Coronary Heart Disease Risk: Prospective Analysis from the Atherosclerosis Risk in Communities (ARIC) Study." *Circulation* 101: 2034–2039.

Williams, Redford B. 1987. "Psychological Factors in Coronary Artery Disease: Epidemiologic Evidence." *Circulation* 76 (Supplement I), I-117.

INDEX

ABOUT THE AUTHORS

RESHMI SIDDIQUE, PH.D.

Reshmi Siddique has a doctorate in epidemiology (public health) from Case Western Reserve University School of Medicine, Cleveland, Ohio. She has a bachelor's degree in economics from The London School of Economics, London University, and a master's degree in economics from Oxford University, England, U.K. Reshmi also obtained a master's degree in health management and policy from The New School for Social Research, New York.

Reshmi has worked as a scientist in various research organizations. She has published extensively in both public health and medical journals, including the *American Journal of Public Health* and *Archives of Internal Medicine*. She has also presented at national conferences.

Reshmi enjoys oil painting as a hobby; she particularly likes to paint seascape sunsets. She lives with her husband, Mahmood, in New Jersey. They have two children: a daughter, Rania, and a son, Ryan.

MAHMOOD SIDDIQUE, D.O.

Mahmood Siddique is a Clinical Assistant Professor of Medicine at the University of Medicine and Dentistry of New Jersey-Robert

Wood Johnson Medical School, New Brunswick. He trained in Pulmonary, Critical Care, and Sleep Medicine at Case Western Reserve University, Cleveland, Ohio. He completed his residency in Internal Medicine at Robert Wood Johnson Medical School. He received his degree from the Midwestern University, Chicago College of Osteopathic Medicine.

Mahmood is the Medical Director of the SleepCare Center at Robert Wood Johnson University Hospital at Hamilton, New Jersey. He is board certified in Internal Medicine, Pulmonary Diseases, Critical Care, and Sleep Medicine. Mahmood received multiple "Excellence in Teaching" awards at Robert Wood Johnson Medical School. He has authored book chapters and many scientific articles in peer-reviewed journals. He was selected to be on the peer-nominated Best Doctors list. Mahmood lectures extensively and routinely appears as a guest speaker on radio and television discussing various health topics.

How to Contact the Authors

The authors can be contacted at the following address:
P.O. Box 6539
Lawrenceville, NJ 08648

GIVE THE GIFT OF
HOW TO TURN ANGER INTO LOVE
TO YOUR FRIENDS

Check Your Local Bookstore or Order Here

❑ YES, I want ____ copies of *How to Turn Anger into Love* for $14.95 each.

Include $4.99 shipping and handling for one book and $2.99 for each additional book. Ohio and New Jersey residents must include applicable sales tax. Canadian orders must include payment in U.S. funds, with 7% GST added. Payment must accompany orders. Allow 2 weeks for delivery.

My check or money order for $ _____ is enclosed.

Please charge my ❑ Visa   ❑ MasterCard   ❑ American Express

Name _____

Organization _____

Address _____

City/State/Zip _____

Phone _____   E-mail _____

Card# _____

Exp. Date _____   Signature _____

CALL (800) 247-6553

Make check payable and return to:
QualHealth Inc.
30 Amberwood Parkway
Ashland, OH 44805
or visit
www.HowToTurnAngerIntoLove.com